The Saint Germain Chronicles Collection

A Journey Into Practical Spirituality

GORDON CORWIN II

Lah Rahn Ananda

Ingram Spark Edition 2016

Volume I

Copyright © 2014 - 2016 Gordon W. Corwin II Lah Rahn Ananda.

ALL RIGHTS RESERVED
INCLUDING THE RIGHT OF REPRODUCTION
IN WHOLE OR IN PART IN ANY FORM.

HIGHLAND LIGHT PUBLISHERS IS
A REGISTERED TRADEMARK
WITH THE U.S PATENT
AND TRADEMARK OFFICE.

GORDON W.
CORWIN II

All rights reserved. No part of this book may be used or reproduced by any means, graphic, electronic, or mechanical, including photocopying, recording, taping or by any information storage retrieval system without the express written permission of the author except in the case of brief credited quotations embodied in critical articles and reviews.

The Saint Germain Chronicles Collection Books may be ordered by visiting the Author's website

www.SaintGermainChronicles.org

or through independent and chain booksellers, libraries, and online retailers worldwide, plus every major e-book retailer (including iBookstore, Kobo, Amazon Kindle, Barnes & Noble Nook), and other Ingram Partners.

Because of the dynamic nature of the U.S Postal system and the Internet, any addresses, web addresses or links contained in this book may have changed since publication and may no longer be valid. The views expressed in this work are conditioned by the Disclaimer which follows. Certain stock imagery © Dreamstime.com, 123RF.com, and Gordon W. Corwin II.

ISBN 978-0-9914924-1-1

Print information is available on the last page.

P.O Box 6007
Oceanside, CA. 92056-6237

DISCLAIMER

The information contained within this Book is strictly for educational purposes. This Book and the Book's elements are provided to readers committed to Spiritual education, self-discovery, self-actualization, and transformation to align individual belief systems with a common source, Our Creator and Spirit, as the guiding light to enter doorways of change, new possibilities, growth, and manifestations within reach of an extraordinary and self-examined Human lifetime. Readers are encouraged to choose, of their own free will and volition, to accept, to follow, or to reject the guidance, ideas, philosophies, stated truths, and techniques presented herein. If you wish to apply ideas and guidance contained herein, you are taking full responsibility for your actions. This Book contains information and general advice that is intended to help the readers to be better informed about physical, mental, emotional, and Spiritual well-being. Always consult your doctor for your individual needs. This Book is not intended to be a substitute for the medical advice of a licensed physician. The reader should consult with their doctor in any matters relating to his/her health. This Book contains information and general advice about business pursuits. This book is not intended to be a substitute for financial or legal advice. Reader is advised to consult your licensed financial or legal professional for such matters. In no event does the author or the Publisher make guarantees, express or implied, as to results or consequences arising out of or related to the reader's use or inability to use the book's contents. Both the author and Highland Light Publishers (the Publisher) do not assume and hereby disclaim any liability to any party for any loss, direct, indirect, or consequential damages, accidental, unintentional, or unforeseen, pain, suffering, emotional distress, or disruption resulting from the reader's negligence, actions or non-actions, accident, or any other cause.

ACKNOWLEDGEMENTS

To All of those who have so generously contributed their loving, timely, and ongoing support to the success of this book, using your unique creative talents and abilities, artistry, technical skills, financial resources, and much more, We Ascended, along with Lah Rahn Ananda, give Our highest appreciation and most grateful praise to You All.

We send special recognition and Blessings to each of you, with acknowledgment of your meaningful contributions toward maximizing the impact of the Wisdom, guidance and teachings We lovingly present for the enlightenment of Humanity. Thank you all for assisting Spirit in bringing these Divinely sourced Chronicles into full bloom and worldwide circulation.

Llantar Chris Gulve and Elaryia Gulve, for your unceasing, loving contributions and encouragement over these many many years, in support of Spirit on Earth, The Saint Germain Chronicles Collection, furthering of Spiritual education, and the Light of the Soul Foundation, with all of their past and future outreach, touching countless numbers of Divining Souls.

Manfred Alther, for Being the fine demonstration you are, as an eager, willing, and receptive student of Spirit and Alchemy, and for your generosity of heart, enthusiasm, and Faith in the true value of the Saint Germain Chronicles. Your dedicated continuing support for the success of this Chronicled Spiritual publishing to benefit Humanity World-wide, is a remarkable tribute to your fine and expanding character as a Spiritual Being.

Marius Michael-George, for the most beautiful licensed, color images of your paintings, presenting likenesses of Ascended Masters Saint Germain and El Morya.
Artwork © Marius Michael-George
www.Mariusfineart.com

Tim Yargeau, with special thanks, for your kind and enthusiastic co-operation in applying your creative and very effective graphic design and photography skills, just when they were most needed! The results of your fine work greatly enhance the true beauty of many graphic displays throughout the book. www.streamlinemediaSD.com

Teri Rider, for the spectacular graphic design and image creation of the Highland Light Monogram and LOGO, banner and all! www.teririder.com

Mark Reichenthal, Esq. for your friendly and capable advice, and your guiding hand in obtaining Trademark and Copyright registrations for Our original artwork and graphic images, and for introducing Us to the stark realities of the Publishing Industry.
www.Branfman.com

Taylor Gallegos, for your willing, tireless and positive artistic energies, which you so patiently and cheerfully applied to illustrations in collaboration with Gordon Corwin, Lah Rahn Ananda.

Dreamstime.com, for your print licensed permission to utilize graphic images that add so much to illustrate text, solely inside the book in various places, with imagination and beauty.
Dreamstime.com

FCIT Florida Center for Instructional Technology, for the licensed use of your copyrighted, beautiful Floral, Ornate, and Decorative capital letters to illustrate text, inside of the book.
licensing@fcit.us

123RF Limited, for your beautiful graphic images, print licensed for Our use, adding so much illustrative vitality in various places, solely inside of the book 123RF.com

Public Domain, for location of the Comte Saint Germain portrait, and the circa 1864 Charles Sindelar public domain original portrait image of Saint Germain.
The Public Domain Review

Additional Acknowledgements appear at end of the book.

Light of the Soul Foundation

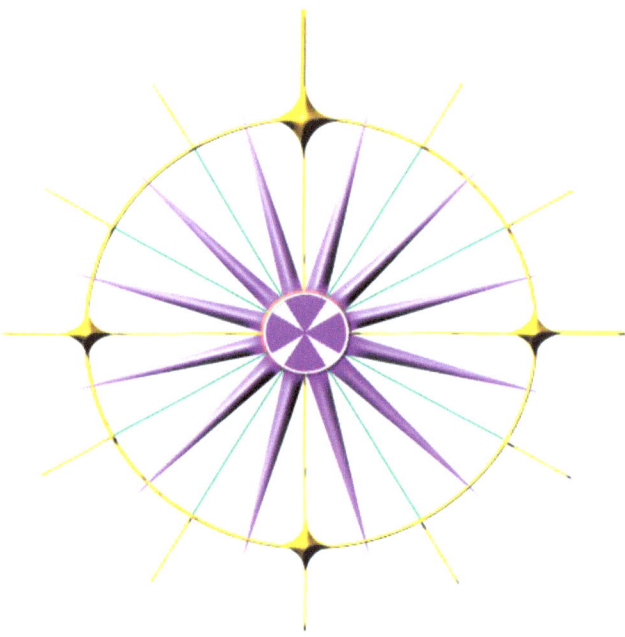

The Light of the Soul Foundation is a philanthropic non-profit 501 (c)(3) charitable organization dedicated to the enlightenment of Humanity through Spiritual education.

Highland Light Publishers is harmoniously bonded with LOSF, sharing this Spiritual mission and facilitating its manifestation through creating, publishing, distributing and delivering written works and live events from the Ascended Masters Above.

Oceanside, CA. 92056

Chronicles@LightoftheSoul.org

GRATITUDE

To My Dear Friends walking your path. As you allow Ascended Spirit to enlighten and expand the veins of your consciousness, I invite you to please join me in reciprocating the deepest possible gratitude for the very wonders of the Creator's Universe itself, and for the infinite brilliance embodied in this interconnecting structure throughout the highest dimensions of Universal Consciousness.

God and Spirit have so ingeniously interwoven, as ONE, an amazing, infinitely organized hierarchical structure of Ascended Beings and timeless wisdom, allowing us on Earth to receive purifying transmissions from Above in real time, as they are continuously and effortlessly sent to Humanity. In my Channelship and role as a Partner of Spirit, I AM most grateful to serve as a minute part of this wondrous network of Spirit and Light, receiving for you the highest vibrational Octaves of Universal Truth. In more simple terms, this is gratefulness for delivery of our Divinely guided tool-set for living 'The Grand Process' in this lifetime of self-transformation, awake and aware.

You may know that individual Ascended Masters carry their own unique energy, style, and color, delivering that segment of the Whole, which is their Ray of assigned specialty. And yet, ironically, these Beings are fully aligned, integrated, amalgamated, and enfolded into the greater Whole as ONE. I AM personally grateful that this demonstration of transcended Oneness from Above displays doorways to Unity consciousness and then God Consciousness for all of us. My dream is for you to find these Chronicles to be your Personal Spiritual Guidebook, leading you to experience the perfection of God's Grace, as you walk through your own doorways arched with inset stones of timeless wisdom.

These Saint Germain Chronicles contain energies emanating from *several* different Ascended Masters to whom I AM immensely grateful. Please join me in the most heartful acknowledgement of: Lords Saint Germain, El Morya, Buddha, Hilarion, Mighty Victory, Jesus Sananda, Lady Portia, Lady Nada, Mother Mary, Archangels Michael, Zadkiel, Gabriel, and countless enlightened Beings, standing to serve when called. May Spirit's Grace gently crown your consciousness as you walk your unique path of discovery and quest into Mastery of this lifetime.

Love and Blessings, Lah Rahn / Gordon Corwin

The Saint Germain Chronicles
Volume I

HIGHLIGHTS AND CONTENTS

Introduction ~ Master El Morya

Soul Evolvement, First Ray of Spirit, Your Pathway, Awareness of Opportunities, Recurring timeless Truths, Practical Spirituality, The Human Condition, The Human Illusion, Blessings of Compassion, Excellence, The 5th Dimension, Mastery.

The Ordinary and the ExtraOrdinary ~ 1st Edition 08-2008

Alchemy and Freedom, Your choice in the balance, Rebellious Ego, The Status Quo, rewards of an examined lifetime, untamed Ego, Human illusion, Change, Beingness, Love and True Wisdom, Understanding vs. Knowing, Life's Lessons, Free-will, The Extraordinary, Hearing the Divine voice.

Openings For Possibility ~ 2nd Edition 04-2011

Your Personal Universe, Partners in Spirit, Open mind, Friend of Change, Your patterns, denial, stuckness, lifted burdens, alternatives, Alignment with Spirit, Aligned behavior examples, proactive power, fear of success, suffering, portrait of the Buddha, perspectives, impossible as possible, Practical guidance, Blessed Openings.

Your Emotions in The White Light ~ 3rd Edition 11-2008

Soul searching, the Emotional challenge, Hope, reflection, Divine Assets, Love and Integrity, recognizing emotional states, emotions and outcomes, moving energy, Faith, fears, action, listen and talk to Your chakras, chakra self-clearings, balancing, Meditation, perseverance, responsibility, healing, purification, Soul Merge.

Blessings of Synchronicity ~ 4th Edition 08-2010

Spirit's touch, The Grand Self, Heartful Devotion, Mastery of Your journey, the Embrace of Synchronicity, first and second births, choice, a "taken" state of Being, Peace, devotion, Your tears, The Question, Synchronicity and Grace delivered, Divine Hosts, Gratefulness, +
Prayer of Divine Moments – Master El Morya.

Mystery of Change ~ 5th Edition 1998-2010

Earth energy shifts, Spiritual armour, tides of change, Mastering Human condition, Being Blissful in the midst of Change, Flight of the Soul, demanding, deserving higher vibrations, The Truth, Protection, access to Spirit, new vibrations, Your personal Universe, religion, Free-will choice - Your centerpiece of Change Your full Partnership with Spirit.

Part 2. Sacred Changes and Freedom

Balance and more light, You are not alone, Duality, Trust in Spirit releases doubt and fear, Accepting what IS, suffering, Grace of healing, Maintaining upper chakras, multi-dimensional Being, Alchemy.

Unity, Separation and Sphere of Truth ~ 6th Edition 08-2008

Shades of Light and Dark, your Internet, misinformation, accountability, Pivotal Free-will Choice, Collective consciousness, personal Sphere of Truth, 3rd Dimensional illusions, illusion draped in Truth, domination, Living life by design vs. Living life by default, shedding Ego parts, Dark religious prophecies, spreading fear, Loving integration of the Whole, Truth and Freedom, Your birthright.

Openings for Opportunity ~ 7th Edition 04-2011

Ascended Masters of Spirit, Library of Heavenly Wisdom, Your Collection, Access to Unconditional Love, Teachings that Beckon, Soul's evolvement, Enlightenment guidelines, pursuit of an examined life, The Grand Process, Imprints of your Soul, Carpe Diem, Examined life pursuits, integrated Wisdom, Flight of the Soul (ref.), Holy Presence Decree.

GOD's Business and Your Free-will ~ 8th Edition 08-2011

God's Will unfolding, dynamic Cosmic energies, separation, blending with Spirit, surrender and Free-will, Archangel Michael, The Divine Voice, Mastery and Your vibration, devotion and expansion of auric field, fully evolved Divine Beings, Pleiadians, Your lifelong test, Free-will Blessing and responsibility, wise daily practices, observe Yourself, humility, The Ascension Process, Flight of the Soul Ascension training book ref., Spiritual observer, Love and Freedom.
+ Tuning Up Your Vibrations.

Growing to Fill Your Divine Business Shoes ~ 9th Edition 02-2012

Spirit in 3rd dimensional business, role of integrity and reputation, balance, growth, White Light energy, reacting in fear, separation, alignment, quintessential ingredient of Spiritual journey, vows of Soul contract, unyielding Ego, hypocrisy, Truth, lifelong tests, nurturing and purifying, Spiritual presence as Your companion, aligned manifestation, Affirmation of Abundance, Our sacred embrace.

Health Matters ~ 10th Edition 02-2013

Top challenge, Physical, Mental, Spiritual well-being Setting life's priorities, distractions, stress behaviors, practices and discipline, merit worthy choices, cleansing body vs. mind, Your comfort zone, Change, regular routine, moment of Truth, health maintenance or breakdown, price of neglect - physical/emotional, extended rewards, health perk joys, Your Temple,

Health Karma. + **Amazing Grace.**

The Manifesting Power of Each Moment ~ 11ᵗʰ Edition 02-2013

Illumination Decree, presence in the moment,
Accepting and caring for Your moments, holding
Your energy by Decree, Om (Aum), Your surrender
in Our Partnership, detachment, outcome, walking in
humble nobility, Alchemy, secular world, radiating
light, You and the Universe, Light and Love.
Access to the Divine Mind, One with the One.

Dealing with your Fluctuating Emotions ~ 12ᵗʰ Edition 08-2013

Raising Your vibration, Soul Searching,
The Human condition, Emotional states, conscious
awareness, Ego, mood management, Harmony,
Buddha of Compassion portrait, lessons of
the Buddha, Transcendental Meditation, quiet mind,
handling emotions one at a time, reacting, heightened
intuition, Spectrum of choices, insights, Free-will,
Portal to higher Realms.

Wisdom Quotations ~ 13ᵗʰ Edition 2004-2013

*The Grand Process * The Truth * Soul Searching*
** Ripe Moments On The Vine * From Above*

Manifestation Magic ~ 14ᵗʰ Edition 07-2014

The Grand Realm of Divine Magic, Earthly
Manifestation, Human endeavors, Marketing
Manifestation elements, conditions of Spirit's
Endorsement, Saint Germain's Stock and Trade,
3ʳᵈ Dimensional plane aspects, Duality, secular
versus Divine framework, Your invitation,
Blessings of Synchronicity, serendipity contrasted,
awakening to Gifts of Grace, Gratitude, the Gaze,
Aligned outcomes, holding the 5ᵗʰ Dimension and higher!

Author Biography

ordon Corwin II, also known as Lah Rahn Ananda, translated literally as 'God Light Messenger', is a native Californian, educated at UC Berkeley, followed by service as a Commissioned US Naval Officer, and by extensive careers in the computer and real estate industries.

In 1995, Gordon clearly heard Lord Saint Germain's resounding and mysterious voice from Above, recruiting him to immediately engage with Ascended Spirit and follow his Soul's calling to reactivate his considerable past life Atlantean DNA channeling abilities, and to begin walking his Dharma to serve Humanity! As an appointed Masters' Representative, Lah Rahn then began delivering Ascended energies through channeling of the Masters' words and visual media, which would now become his changed and conscious life path. In 1998 he founded The Light of the Soul Foundation, a qualified non-profit entity for advanced Spiritual education and Human philanthropy.

Following years of ego-cleansing by the Masters, Lah Rahn Ji has, for 17 years now, delivered clear and engaging channelings of public and private Spiritual events along with potent and enlightening mentoring of Chelas in The Light of the Soul Vortex in Southern California.

In 2007 he was highly honored to be chosen by Lord Saint Germain to be the Ascended Masters' instrument and Partner to begin, and later complete, this precise and accurate channeling to Earth of

The Saint Germain Chronicles Collection, 2008-2016.

Lah Rahn's Adventure

What more would you like to know about the Author?

Lah Rahn Ananda is an Ascended Masters' Channel representing Divine Realms of the Holy Spirit as he channels down to Earth their energies, discourses, dictations, and illustrative pictures, all bringing in the Violet Flame and White Light of *practical Spirituality* to incarnated Souls of the Earth-world. In this role, he does public speaking, private and public channeling, counseling, and authors numerous published works. This latest publishing, *The Saint Germain Chronicles Collection*, continues to source those who *truly choose to be chosen* and to further their self-discovery, self-actualization, Spiritual evolvement and Ascension process.

The name Lah Rahn Ananda means "Serene God Light Messenger-Teacher", a literal translation surprisingly revealed years ago by a Buddhist Monk visiting in Encinitas, California.

His favorites include harmony, oceans and lakes, water sports, aqua marine colors, sailing, animals, loving relationships, music and playing the acoustic guitar, manifestation, and the Will of God. (and…Flyfishing). He is known for his grounded Light, good nature, and special gifts for teaching and writing, especially about the practical aspects of individually understanding and applying the Ascended Masters' wisdom. Lah Rahn is said by some to embody the essences of several Ascended Masters including those of Saint Germain and El Morya.

Lah Rahn, as he is known in the Spirit world, has been an enthusiastic, loyal and relentless seeker of Universal Truth and a devoted student of personal evolvement since 1982, when he first learned that this would become his highest priority lifelong pursuit "from there on in." Soon to follow, he joined in with self-actualization training groups, the EST training, Ayurvedic disciplines, and years of *how-to seminars* from earth "gurus" who *claimed and said* they knew "how to."

And then one summer day in 1994, Gordon Corwin, soon to become Lah Rahn Ananda, was contacted directly by the Holy Spirit and was spoken to by Saint Germain in particular, and loudly informed that "Now YOU belong To Me". A real jolt!

There was no mistake about the identity of the booming voice from above or the source.

Lah Rahn's dormant Atlantean channeling abilities were being reactivated.

This stunning announcement, along with an unnerving jolt of Divine Light, was spark enough to quickly ignite his desire to *know* more about the essence of Spirit. As this enthusiasm continued, he became a persevering, relentless devotee of Spirit, ravenously hungry for Universal Law, Divine Truth, and seeking growth into One who could somehow apply all of this in every day Earth-life.

For a left-brained, 25 year businessman at the time, holding a B.S. degree from the University of California at Berkeley, this was a real shocker. After much internal kicking and screaming, resistance, skepticism, and Ego struggling, the only next step (beyond a somewhat agnostic belief) was to move *Upward*. Lah Rahn was then "Mysteriously" drawn to a presentation in Laguna Beach, where somehow it was Master Saint Germain speaking through another channel on that day. This was only 2 weeks after almost *losing his life* hiking on the cliff face of Bell rock in Sedona, Arizona. Needless to say, being miraculously "saved" from a dangerous 30 foot fall, acutely *heightened* his willingness to listen attentively when an Ascended Master was speaking directly to him!

In 1995 Gordon Corwin, now Lah Rahn, began to directly and clearly hear lengthy Spiritual dissertations,…energies (transformed into words) of the Ascended Masters and Angelic Kingdom. Soon thereafter, he was requested to undergo rigorous, sometimes lovingly ruthless, *channelship training*. Upon completion of this training some years later, Lah Rahn was Divinely licensed and invited by the Ascended Masters to speak directly to public audiences with dissertations, spoken live from all the Masters, as they came into and through him. He says his own personal challenges immediately included staying focused and "*walking the talk as it's taught.*"

Then came the assignment of channeling years of public Spiritual events and classes in the San Diego and Los Angeles areas, along with bringing through what would later amount to many hundreds of written transmissions of the Ascended Masters, Archangels, and their Realms. Many of these works are now in print and soon to be E-books published Worldwide.

Audiences and private Spiritual students alike find Lah Rahn to be enthusiastic and clear, while he heartfully works and speaks and writes *about the Ascended Masters' higher vibrational teachings for the enlightenment of Divining Chelas, Devotees and Light Workers,* and yet, he still comes across as "grounded" to deliver accurate channeled etherical energies of practical healing for the growth and evolvement of aspiring Souls.

His continued unveilings of enlightening and closely-held Truths (and Myths) of the Mystery School bring joy and White Light to individuals, Spiritual groups, and audiences alike … all part of non-denominational Spiritual teachings that surround Lah Rahn. He continues to deliver books and the channeled words of the Ascended Masters to an expanding cluster of Light Workers, Chela devotees, and Truth seekers. Lah Rahn is the founder of The Light of the Soul Foundation and Highland Light Publishers.

Although unique Spiritual energies of many different Ascended Masters and Archangels are sent to Lah Rahn to be channeled on Earth, Masters Saint Germain, El Morya, Archangel Michael and Mighty Victory most frequently appear for their vibrations to be precisely and colorfully expressed, both verbally and written in English. In particular, Ascended Master Saint Germain, as Maha Chohan of the Aquarian Age, has chosen to viscerally indwell within Lah Rahn's consciousness for the past 19 Earth years … for which he is Grateful.

Now, living as a Multi-dimensional Being … the way his life has turned out, … Lah Rahn devotes time and energy to enjoying life, serving the Ascended Masters, being an Author, traveling, making music, and working in the secular "Earth World" in North County San Diego, California as a Management Consultant, serving clients in the USA and Europe.

Devoted Spiritual Channels on Earth, such as Lah Rahn, among others, are unique Demonstrations of **DIVINE ALCHEMY**, where the Sacred fire energy of Holy Spirit above is blended with the visceral DNA helix spiral of an altered and expanded consciousness in a Human Being.
This form of **ALCHEMY** is delivered in Divine service to Humanity by

Lah Rahn / Gordon Corwin

"Ripe Moments On the Vine"

AFFIRMATION FOR YOUR HARVEST

"I AM joyfully *willing* to love, care for and accept each new moment of My life as it unfolds. I acknowledge *'what is'*, and embrace the swinging door of *choice* to transcend *My* old and burdensome *judgments*.

My *life's purpose is* integrated with a clear vision of *'Change' as* inevitable, ... empowering Me with the Freedom to lead an *extraordinary examined life that is worth living.*"

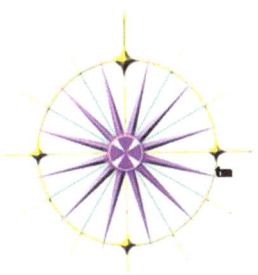

Lah Rahn / Gordon Corwin 10-2013

The Saint Germain Chronicles Collection

INTRODUCTION

Spoken by

EL MORYA

 gratefully come unto you this fine day at the request of Blessed Ascended Master Saint Germain, to introduce to you this brilliant enlightening Collection of Saint Germain Chronicles which you now hold in your hands.

Within, you shall find your invitation to accept Our grand gift, nurturing the highest and finest evolvement of your Earthly and Spiritual Self, as you blaze your trail and walk the cobblestones of your pathway toward achieving the extraordinary excellence of your Soul's evolvement, through courageously living an examined lifetime in intimate and harmonious Partnership with Spirit.

I AM Ascended Master El Morya, holder of the First Ray of Spirit, The Will of God. In My role, I lovingly hold your heart in My hands, as I usher you into this first Volume of *Divinely Chronicled guidance*, sourced and energized by Blessed Ascended Master Saint Germain, the God-gifted *Spiritual* author of these Chronicles and your Spirit guide through this wisdom-filled Journey into Practical Spirituality, focused upon essential *Keys for Self-transformation.*

At long last, after many years of dictations and transmissions from the Spirit World, these spectacular works are humbly and gratefully revealed to *You*, the inquiring and dedicated One, awaiting heightened *discovery of your true Soul-self,* and the *expansion of your Being,* here and now. We in the Ascended Realm, fully hold you in Our affectionate embrace, sourcing you beyond the resistance and fears of unknown personal heights you may achieve by opening your awareness to *yet unseen possibilities and opportunities for this lifetime.* Our energies have been lovingly channeled to Earth, diligently gathered and assembled with great love and care for you during the Earth year period of 2008 – 2014.

Although Truth is timeless, the long list of recurring topics which We Ascended have chosen to address in this Collection is, nonetheless, timely now and in dire need of your attention, as you will soon discover. These crucial and poignant issues, *indigenous to the Human Condition*, seem to confront and challenge you and yours, individually and collectively, at this particular space/time interval of your Earth years.

The Central focus of addressing the Human Condition and hence the *evolvement of your consciousness* in this one present lifetime on Earth is, simply said, for you to pierce and crack the veil of the Human Illusion. That is it in a nutshell, Dear Friends! Your *choice to allow* this process is in your hands alone. WE Ascended fully embrace and actively support affirmative Human choices to engage, … and to *willingly allow the sequential unfoldment* of this individual life-long process, be it launching now or continuing.

Discovering the Human Illusion, and wrapping your full Self around all of its facets, is indeed an ongoing part of this "Grand Process", as more Light enters your Being and as Mastery reveals it's loving face.

Then, Mastering the Human Illusion, ironically enough, goes hand in hand with it's very *discovery*! By you! Be not surprised that pursuing "The Grand Process", discussed and clearly illustrated within these Chronicles, requires your unwavering dedication.

Calling forth certain personal qualities, challenging as they may be, will assist you greatly and forge your progress onward! The list includes acceptance, dedication, perseverance, self-love, humor, detachment, joy, … and more, as you will soon discover in your *Journey into Practical Spirituality,* where these Chronicles lovingly hold your brave heart and Divining Soul along your Dharmic path.

As written within the many Editions to follow, Saint Germain embraces and brings *into the Light* a wide range of current-day and yet age-old topics, all so very essential in your everyday dealings with the *Human Condition*, its reality, its challenges and, of course, its rewards when the Mastery is merged in union with Spirit by the Multidimensional Being You aspire to Be.

In brief, this *Saint Germain Chronicles Collection* is a mighty and prodigious wellspring of Spiritual Wisdom and Truth, best described as *Practical Spirituality*. Our intention is to guide you effectively in pursuing and conquering your life's lessons and manifesting personal *breakthroughs*, melded and spun into the Grand Process of an *extraordinary, examined, and joyful Earthly lifetime, Blessed with countless Synchronicities and laced with Ease and Grace*.

Spirit brings you *Blessings of Compassion*, as you and your brethren move through this *Grand Process of evolvement*. We acknowledge your vulnerable willingness to inquire into and re-choose with Free-will among the *vast possibilities for enriching your current* life incarnation by opening the pages of this book, knowing full well that jolting changes in your belief system may be afoot.

As students of Spirit soon discover, consciously sorting out the many aspects of the *Human Condition, although humorous at times,* becomes a daunting task. This We acknowledge. Therefore, We offer here *Our guidance*, to more easily enable your choice of Spiritual solutions, as you walk your walk along the path of your own unique Dharma, in Divine Partnership with Ourselves, versus *attempting* to "go it alone".

As you proceed to consciously recognize, experience, and then Master the seemingly unceasing flood of life-lessons knocking and sometimes pounding at your door, *patience* becomes paramount in your journey up the Spiritual ladder of life. *New Building Blocks* lay grounding fundamentals for a firm foundation *to expand your consciousness*, … all carefully presented and fastidiously delineated throughout these Editions, … directing your focus *to hone, polish, and purify behaviors, … to smooth out the rough edges!* Throughout, Saint Germain *embraces you with energies of love, empowerment, and compassion*, in concert with Universal and Divine Law, guiding you to enthusiastically allow your *Grand Process* adventure of this Earthly lifetime to run its course with expanded ease and grace and Spiritual upliftment.

My Sweet Ones, I entreat you to willingly follow this advice I now offer to you regarding how best to go about reading and viewing the *Chronicles* in your mind's eye: hold the examples of Human behavior discussed herein not as criticisms, but as valuable lessons which may truly apply to your life-stream, and consequently *point the way to a* constructive restructuring of your choices of behavior through *empowering refinements to your belief system, however humbling this Process may be!*

I recognize that you may choose to regard *change* as painful, and yet, if you are wise, you will soon *learn to regard certain changes* within your Personal Universe as necessary and some as inevitable for your evolvement and ultimately for your well-being.

So, in your own *Process,* why not create passion fused with joy and excitement about the very adventure of this life itself, Divinely seducing your resistance into surrender, as you make *change your Friend!* On the lighter side, your game of life has its winners!

For further reinforcement, We strongly advise that you carefully read through and absorb your *Chronicles in a special way:* know that you will *best serve yourself to remember, as you turn pages,* that these same pages will need to be "re-turned", *reread and reread again*, possibly ad infinitum, to facilitate your full understanding, and *later your full knowing* of what is said! *It's part of the Grand Process.* So, I beseech you to reward yourself with the Blessings of your own perseverance, determination and patience, which surely await your action.

From Saint Germain's light-infused energies to follow, your heightened consciousness and awareness can source and lead you toward open doors of Mastery of the *Human Condition*, along with the joy and peace that is *possible to be yours in this single lifetime* of achievable Excellence. Yes, Our standards are high, believe Me!

Be reassured, that ultimately a consciousness integrated in love, truth, and wisdom, is destined to enjoy sweet rewards of the low hanging fruit of life in your Earth-world. I assure you, from personal experience leading to *my own Ascension*, that along with your challenges, countless Earthly and Spiritual pleasures await, … pending *your full engagement, as you now turn the pages* <u>of your lifetime</u> *from this moment forward.*

<u>*As you navigate your path, may your journey be filled with sweetness and joy, combined with the Mystery of Change, Marvelous Synchronicities, Emotions in the White Light, Perfect Health, Unity with Truth, Growing to Fill Your Divine Business Shoes, and Aligned Manifestations of Alchemy beyond your fondest dreams.*</u>

Our intention for you, in the stride of your life's-process, is for you to reach the highest vibrational plane possible for a Human consciousness. And to join Us in Our Realm! Let your reach for the 5th Dimension and higher vibrations be your goal, if that be your next step. Ultimately, your *full evolution* shall yield bountiful rewards, connecting and merging your Earthly-consciousness with your Soul-self, and in turn, merging with the Divine Mind and The All of All. This is the Blessed Soul Merge, Dear Ones!

I hold you in My arms with fondest Blessings, in the Light of God, Spirit, and in the highest aspirations for your Soul. Your Faith and Devotion will surely lead your walk to include a *Multi-dimensional reality and a true freedom*, through an Extraordinary examined lifetime seeking Mastery and Enlightenment.

In the highest octave of vibration holding the Will of God,

I AM
EL MORYA

*Channeled through
Lah Rahn Ananda
03-30-2014*

Acknowledgement
Portrait by MariusFineArts

A New Perspective

Acknowledgement
Sketch by TayloredArts

Congratulations !

In this 1st Volume of the Saint Germain Chronicles, you shall discover and be Blessed with a wealth of Truth. Herein, practical guidance from the Ascended Masters is delivered to the doorstep of your personal Universe.

These timeless Truths can be integrated into your everyday life's consciousness, ultimately rendering peace, joy, and Freedom through your newly acquired emotional balance, aligned and in tune with Ascended Spirit's guidance and Universal Law.

Enjoy your Saint Germain Chronicles journey, while you carefully navigate using this precious gift which you now hold in your hands.

Blessings and Light,

Saint Germain and Lah Rahn Ananda

The Saint Germain Chronicles Collection

Volume I

The Ordinary
and the
Extraordinary

Acknowledgement
Charles Sindelar
Public Domain, Original Portrait circa 1864

ow observe clearly, that the life's lessons of an "ordinary unexamined Human life" are often dramatized, elongated and most commonly amplified by a strong and rebellious EGO consciousness, lamentably and inextricably attached to a belief system that adores the status quo. These Chronicles are about transcending into the Extraordinary Realms that await!

Unfortunate attachment that would <u>resist</u> uplifting Change and its consequent potential for evolvement and enlightenment, is destined to rotate around and around on the Karmic wheel, ad infinitum, until the cycle may be broken, I pray. Thus, as you shall soon discover, all *14 Essential Keys to Transformation* embraced throughout these Chronicles carry a common thread of Spirit's <u>empowerment</u> for you to tame the Ego and consciously evolve as I guide you along.

Read on my good and curious friends.

Untrained and swept up by its drama and illusionary importance of itself, this untamed EGO would forever rule as King in an unexamined Human lifetime that could otherwise be re-trained, aligned with Spirit, … to include **ALCHEMY and FREEDOM**, … and finally be amalgamated into a Soul, ready to blend harmoniously with surrender into Love and Light … a joyous win-win style of Earth-living, thus prepared to Ascend into the Heart of GOD.

Such a courageous surrendering of One's old belief system, set in place by an untrained EGO during such an unexamined Human lifetime, is a remarkably courageous act on your part, as a Divining One who has "heard their own call". The energies of the Realm of Ascended Masters appear here, to answer this call to be with you now.

And if you choose otherwise, dear Reader, your elated EGO shall indeed have its own way, to continue on and perhaps later reconsider My offers.

And all of this **EXTRAORDINARY TOPIC** I now bring, My fine feathered friends, is of which to you I now wish to speak!

Your Choice to walk up the **Ascension path** and to pass through the Violet Flame of healing transmutation with every cell in your several bodies … is now at hand. This would be a walk We in Spirit have taken long long ago. It is a walk through the EGO humbling initiations of fire, water and mist of which you have not seen the likes … until, of course, you realize you are presently in the midst of it all, and somehow doing fine!

At this point, you would be well advised to hang on tightly to my boot straps with all of your might!

Self-honoured with this Blessed choice of consciousness training, the awakening Plebe thirsts in search of the illuminating Truth of this lifetime, a drama ongoingly displayed and *acted out upon the revolving stage of your life.*

This "choice in the balance" awaits your call. The call to action is now resting squarely upon your shoulders, oh Blessed students of Spirit who read My dictation. The Millennium has begun!

In your very path, here is your courageous choice entwined in the birth of a miracle of Grace … the Blessing of learning to hear the Divine Voice for yourself, gaining access to the Ascended Masters' Guidance … miracles which stand ready to be called unto your side.

Your extraordinary choice to walk for the rest of this natural lifetime through this Violet Flame portal … into the extraordinary realms … is another quintessential element of your life's process. What will you choose?

NOTA BENE! The <u>untamed</u> Ego will fiercely <u>resist a choice of Extraordinary change</u>!

New realities involving Divine Truth and emotional behavior of Love and Light are very threatening to an Ego that "knows it is always right", insisting on the status quo. Further dark entanglements surface, when greed, corruption, and cruel domination of others lay dense shadows on an EGO, overtaking the potential which aligned Free-will and Grace can bring!

But, once you internalize the Truth of Spirit into your heart, many of the commonly supposed secular facts, figures, and so called "knowledge" thus far in your 3rd Dimensional world, will fade into the dusk. Believe Me. Many of your books, practices, and much of your belief system will fade away, as the discarded parts of your Ego **become superseded by Beingness in the Sphere of Universal Truth, far beyond the Human illusion! Contemplate this!**

And upon Earth, TRUE Wisdom need be regarded as knowledge plus experience wrapped inside of the TRUTH! Ignorance would exclude Truth from the equation!

Yes, these enigmas are part of the Mystery of Miracles I refer to in many of My transmissions. A mouthful to swallow, I realize. More food for your contemplation! Clear your plate!

You must realize, "understanding" will become the booby prize for last place, as you would say! This old part of your highly prized Ego will shed its skin, as a snake sheds an old skin, no longer needed or wanted. The Mystery of Miracles stands on its own, folks.

The **Mystery of Spirit** needs to be embraced and "known" by your loving energies rather than mentally sought after as a "thing" to be understood. **This is a fundamental axiom**. Oh, how many have traveled this road of demanding to understand and ended up with their chariot wheel in a wagon rut, never to be extricated … or should I say exhumed, in this lifetime?

<u>Yes, this change of consciousness is a leap of faith</u> for newcomers and initiates alike. Just know that in your good time, evidences of Blessings in your life will very mysteriously surface from … you know not where. These Blessings will bear just the perfect Synchronicities, in the very moments that they do indeed manifest for you.

Faith, my good lads and lassies, in your Extraordinary future!

Ask My experienced Instruments. They will tell you first hand of their experiences with the Ascended Masters … of Mystery, Grace, Initiations, Joy, Pain, and <u>Lessons.</u>

Only after you have surrendered fully unto the Heart of Spirit and to the Laws of the Universe as part of your moment to moment living, … will you fully know what I mean. So have cheer for possible future Blessings of Grace from all your surrendered efforts, My dear Friends!

"When" … is up to you.

I heartfully invite you to leap unto and into this portal! And, if you will allow Me the honour, I shall be your humble guide from My lair above in this Sacred and ALL important walk.

If you would, however, decline or lack a disciplined wisdom of the moment, then so shall go this extraordinary initiation I offer. And with this, each new moment's lesson, "escorted proudly" by your immovable EGO, will escape your Soul's grasp, and will no doubt be promptly *wafted as the wind sweeps*. I grant your Free-will all of the rope it needs to hang itself!

You shall, of course, have always My extended hand in an open offer of loving and transmutational assistance, should your softening Ego later see the Light and opt out to reconsider. Many vacillate for a time. That is quite understandable. The opportunity is squarely yours, Blessed Students.

You shall not be judged if you decline.

I must warn you that you shall, nonetheless, be handed the lesson of each circumstance as your Blessing. Karma will have its way!

In time, the awakened student is able to count these Blessings in ironic appreciation, as the accumulating incidents of a life's *Dharma* are consciously and willingly chosen to be <u>allowed as lessons</u> AND then to be Mastered as well. Otherwise, you and We just have more and more coping ad nauseam with just another <u>Ordinary unexamined Human lifetime</u>. Oh My!

Integration of love, wisdom, power and rightful domination <u>for the highest good</u>, under the white and *most radiant light of Divine Will*, is the frame of consciousness that I pray for you to achieve. (Other beings incarnated in form have done so! Earthlings take heed!)

Then … We can move mountains together as Co-creators in full Partnership. I know, Ego surrender is a tall order. That is why you are "Tall Souls"!! So take heart lads and lassies. Be ready for the miracles that you ask for … when the ball is thrown your way!!

And then, of course, comes the ongoing dedication and perseverance of choice to keep on passing through the Violet Flame of Change and healing transmutation We offer … day by day. Meditation and singing bowls and deep breathing, please.

May patience be your partner.

Alright. Now, I say to you as well … that Earth portals of opportunity have both an opening and a closing. I urge you from Above, with all of My Wisdom, to fully and carefully examine each of your Divinely offered portals from a Highest-Self perspective, … from a wise altitude, before you choose to enter or to refrain!

You will also have realization upon pondering my words that this process also carries an implicit <u>training mission</u> in your use of FREE-WILL. This is the bonus plan, as you would say, which I include with My offer!

I AM the guide of choice for many of you. Please know that I honour my Ascended colleagues as well, should they choose to work with you at this juncture in My place until you are ready for My energies again.

So for now, however, give Me your individual and undivided attention. Listen accurately and obey my instructions of Love and Wisdom and you can bypass some of your otherwise thorny, worldly snares.

Yes, I dispense Divine Blessings ongoingly to My devoted Students of Spirit. I pray that you learn to consciously recognize Our Blessings (unexplained miracles, as you might say) in the very moment they are brought unto you. Your gratefulness will be heard.

Elevate your Soul journey, Sweet Ones, onto higher roads … and into higher portals of the …

Extraordinary

Realms **W**here **F**reedom **S**hall

Ring!

I AM in your service

Saint Germain

Channeled in Partnership with
Lah Rahn Ananda

Acknowledgement
Marius Fine Arts

Post Script

To continue, Dear Ones, …
Mark My words. With your Partnership, I will make visible for you extraordinary doors of your *Dharma*. These are the destined, beloved and extraordinary portals of opportunity of which I speak.

The when and where and how this walk of entry is begun, dear Chelas, is part and parcel of the Mastery. <u>You need to seize these essential elements in every opportunity and every lesson.</u>

> **When Mastered, your attained Wisdom will be unveiled before the Lords of Karma, *as the lovely Light of your Soul for All to see.* And I shall be your proud sponsor and etherical Father! … as I, in turn, serve that Father of ALL in the Highest Octave of this Universe.**

Many of you believe I will walk your walk for you. This is false. This is a common myth. Egos sometimes say or are erroneously taught:

'Just ask Saint Germain, he will live your life for you and make your Free-will choices for you'.

'Saint Germain will materialize all that I need'

'Just ask Saint Germain to do it!'

'Then I can just be at my leisure … a dream I've always had.'

'Finally, someone else can take responsibility for my life and make my decisions for me!'

Some Mystery schools are known to teach this myth, it saddens Me to say. *Choose wisely the teachers you engage, dear Ones!* You and you alone bear your *Soul's contract* responsibility for your Human journey and attendant choices of Free-will in your affiliations. Be wise, be careful, and choose your Earth mentors wisely, My friends! There can be an immense cost in mistakes!

Now, … the wise FREE-WILL choice will emanate from a true heart-mind dialogue with your Highest Self, … once you have learned to access this most wonderful part of the real person you are struggling to discover. In addition to My writings, stepping into your own ability to hear directly Our words is so urgently important for your future well-being and evolvement! Time, diligence and dedication yield marvelous results, dear Chelas. Your progress can take a snail's pace or the path of a rocket ship … as you may choose … to create and mold your life's choices to fulfill your destiny of Dharma.

Kindly, re-read for your benefit all of this transmission, including My Post Script, *several times through*, as new meanings will *mysteriously jump out for you, new words from these very same pages!* Mystical it shall be!

Remember that I AM your guide, while you, as the walker, are choosing your walk.

I assist you in footsteps of alignment, and yet still, these footsteps must be yours, for neither I nor collective Spirit are licensed to take your footsteps for you, or We would be walking your walk. In this Age, We Ascended caringly serve Earth World Humans who are in willing quest of an EXTRAORDINARY lifetime, leading toward their magnificent Soul merge and ultimately to their ASCENSION into the arms of Spirit and the Father of ALL, embodied or transitioned, as the case may be.

Ascended Masters have completed their walks in planetary and Cosmic Worlds. We culminated these journeys in Ascension and Freedom some time ago. Such culmination is My everlasting love-filled wish for you.

I AM
Saint Germain
Through Iah Rahn Ananda

08-30-08, 06/2000, 1/14/2004, 04/16/2008, 09/2009, 01/20/2012, 10/11/2013

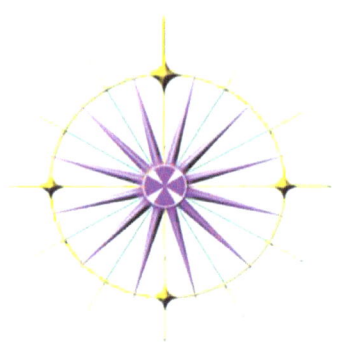

Soul Celebration Decree

I AM in God
God is in Me
God is in Me
I AM in God
I AM in God

God is in Me
God is in Me
I AM in God
God is in Me

repeat 12 times

~ I Am One With the Universe ~

Saint Germain conveys practical guidance sourcing powerful behavior and manifestation basics.

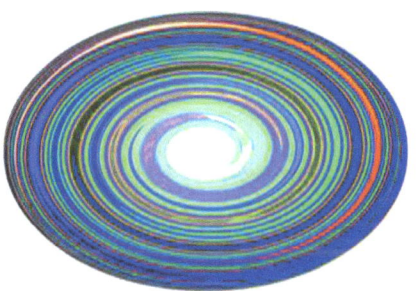

I come to you once again in benevolence and love, My Dear Friends. Your struggles and recent calls for assistance are heard daily in the Ascended Realm, which I now fully embrace, as Master Chohan of the Aquarian Age.

In this transmission, short and to the point as it shall be, I shall assist you in *adopting a path of ease and grace* as you walk nearer to Spirit and become a regular visitor and guest at

My Crystal Cave of Light.

Spirit's intention here is, as always, to *light the walkway of your Dharma,* and to deliver you into openings for new possibilities, sourced by creative and practical use of new habit patterns, adoptable as permanent fixtures in your expanding consciousness. Openings for possibility abound, Dear Friends, and We stand ready as Partners in Spirit along side of you in your intended <u>aligned</u> *visions, plans, actions, and manifestations that shall surround your Personal Universe, as a subset of Our Grand Spiritual Forum of Light.*

As you walk now, I urge you to adopt your "New Self" through a surrender from within to gain access to new Freedoms that My guidance will deliver if you follow My instructions. This is the Aquarian Age of new beginnings, Folks. Observe in your Earth-world the beginnings of dismantling old obsolete structures of learned customs, habits, and procedures and frail integrity, in favor of rebuilding personal and civil foundations that desperately need to be recreated. Here, within these writings, are scribed valuable tools for your Spiritual toolbox.

You hold the power to embrace My invitations of Truth *with open-minded* Thinking, Being, and Doing!

My Dearest friends upon Earth, I entreat you to lay aside your concerns and reservations, and trust in Me. So, … along We go now!

Many of My recent and past transmissions have addressed the ever present phenomenon of CHANGE, a reality that distresses even the best of you at times.

And yet, I must compliment those who have become flexible in <u>surrendering to CHANGE as a routine behavior</u>. Burdens are lifted en masse yes? I KNOW YOU ARE CAPABLE.

And, as you might have learned by now, such an adaptable, surrendered way of Being involves using your GOD given and unique … to this Universe … Human Free-will choice mechanism. Appreciate your gift, as a Human. It is rare in this Universe of Beings.

So it follows, then, that to become a *Friend of Change* is to freely make modifications to your habit patterns, thinking, actions, and your other *aligned* behaviors in support of your Spiritual growth and also a more joyful 3rd Dimensional, secular every day life upon Earth.

Alright. Join with Me now in Choosing to be sourced by your new <u>Proactive behavior</u> -- Using your *creativity, intuition, the Divine guidance I provide to you.* Observe some <u>guidelines:</u>

Committing your whole Self to Our Divine Partnership.

Defining, clearly and distinctly, your *aligned* intended outcome.

Using your Powers to feel, intuit and think "outside of the BOX."

Openly embracing the <u>seemingly impossible</u> as *possible*.

Plowing new turf, exploring creative <u>possibilities that serve.</u>

Empathizing with the perspectives of *Other Peoples' Realities … and distinct from your Personal Universe.*

Humbly combining new possibilities with known circumstances!

Skillfully melding aligned 3rd Dimensional Free-will choices with Divine resources, which We make available to you.

Yes, My Friend, before you ask, I know that swallowing all of this is a tall order in one meal. And choking is not an option.

May I share a secret?

Upon your Earth plane, your manifestation and success

depends upon this, among other factors, …

Making Proactive Choices and Taking Actions to *actually apply creative solutions* for

THAT WHICH IS WANTED AND NEEDED!!

Reflect upon My words for a moment.

…

Now, here is the corollary,

The ~ Magic ~ you can bring to yourself.

Making Proactive Choices and taking Actions, All the while,

Living your <u>focused intention</u>

in harmony with a truly surrendered and <u>heartfelt detachment to the outcome.</u>

<u>**This is your Master Guideline, Folks.**</u>

<u>**These are sacred lessons of the Buddha.**</u>

Acknowledgement:
Photo of carving by Tim Yargeau

Then, of course, there are your alternatives, and My omitting to mention this would be a disservice to a wise, choosing Chela of Spirit: *Certain Alternative Human choices*, **involving Karma, can result in <u>self-induced</u> suffering in different categories, a huge ransom from your quality of life and your growth. Staying** *stuck* **is also your Choice, sourced by:**

<u>**Reactive behavior**</u> **-- Fed by your FEAR OF CHANGE, and failure to deal with fear itself, overlooking the** *power to heal.*

Simple "Denial". Need I say more about reality?

Allowing your <u>fear of CHANGE</u> …. as many will perceive a risk.

Rewarding an *<u>addiction to pain and suffering</u>* by avoiding change.

Staying *Stuck* (We see this often, <u>as one of your habits of choice</u>).

Choosing procrastination <u>as the easy, lazy "way out."</u>

<u>**Suffering about suffering, and suffering about change.**</u>

Fear of what you do NOT know, and of being deceived.

Choosing self-sabotage due to fear <u>of success</u> and all that it brings. Heed lessons of the Buddha about suffering!

Old tapes, and Old habits that don't work, and surrounding negativity.

Ego's pride and closed-minded resistance to Reality, etc.

** *Rejecting the possibility of what is possible!*

Sakyamuni Buddha of Compassion

© Copyright 2014 Gordon W. Corwin II. All rights reserved. Contact: Chronicles@LightoftheSoul.org

Stuckness is a pattern that sometimes adheres to a Chela, <u>unaware</u> of a particular behavior, until it surfaces. Once recognized and when awareness is raised, this <u>pattern can be broken</u> and healed, applying aligned proactive behaviors, yielding a higher and lasting vibrational energy. Absolute self-honesty and discipline, devoid of excuses, must prevail here.

We pray this *new vibration* will indeed stick to you with Cosmic Glue, never to part. We in the Realm applaud you all <u>as you relentlessly dance your way through this Human lifetime of constant change and challenge</u> and surrender unto your highest Soul-self consciousness.

I heartfully invite you to <u>proactively</u> pass through all of your Blessed openings for Possibility and Opportunities when offered in this Age of Possibilities, and to forever adopt your "New Self" upon this very merry day. BE humble and wise enough to accept that YOU *are still a* <u>Student</u> *of your chosen occupation and a humble Student of this Lifetime!*

Experts win last place!

PROMISE YOURSELF THIS GIFT:

To Apply these Principles and Realities

unto your daily life, no matter what!

This is your simple, daily check list!

Let Me know of your progress, Beloved Ones.

In Light I AM,

Saint Germain

Through Lah Rahn Ananda 04-08-11

Can you name some Possibilities Both Inside and Outside of the Box?

Acknowledgement: Painting: TayloredArts Graphic: Tim Yargeau

© Copyright 2014 Gordon W. Corwin II. All rights reserved. Contact: Chronicles@LightoftheSoul.org

Your Emotions in the White Light

In Earth times of massive social Change, Human emotions will predictably run rampant. Of these, fear is the most pronounced, coupled with greed. When most Humans are afraid, they desperately cling to the Status Quo. Likewise, fear of Change in mankind is the oldest emotional challenge, plaguing you in survival and equally in the pursuit of higher consciousness into the white Light of God for those who choose to be chosen. Every incarnated Soul has this Divine opportunity to be chosen. We, in Spirit, nurture, love, and support all to step up to the line to be counted. Many are asked, and few rise to the occasion, answer the call, or take needed action, which is the *worthy companion* of hope.

Soul Searching

In those dreamy and solitary moments of reflection, contemplate .... if you dare

What comes first, the Thought or the Feeling?

o

Who AM I under the mask I wear?

o

What is the focus of My Self-talk?

o

What is the Color of The Truth?

o

Rest assured, Dear Ones, your contemplations and musings are held in the vault of My Heart in the utmost confidence. Embrace your evolving reflections, as they occur over time, in your emerging and unique Grand Process. Blessings in the Light,

El Morya *through Lah Rahn Amanda 2013*

In this transmission, I would like to address the chakra energy centers of your body which can be cleared, balanced and purified such that white light can manifest in and around your crown chakra, the highest of the chakra vibrations that allow you access to cosmic consciousness. These 7 energy centers need to remain clear and open to function in concert with Ourselves in Spirit, and with the Father of ALL. Certain emotions can block these chakras and prevent you from accessing the Divine realms that are your Dharma as well as your birthright.

So, to begin with, let us work with a wide range of typical emotions that directly affect the condition of your body chakras e.g.,

In order to purify, you must know what impurities you are intending to cleanse in this focused cathartic process.

As I have said in earlier transmissions, fear and greed are the two primary emotions that react to CHANGE, which is massive on your Earth at this juncture. However, there is a wide range of Human emotions that accompanies these two. This scale of emotions can play like musical notes in your body, and often not in harmony! Sometimes they play in sequence as I describe below, sometimes pleasing, and at other times they play "the same old discordant tune" every time that particular Change comes up for you. These emotional notes can play in unpredictably random orders that you have never experienced before, sometimes striking chords that cause you much alarm and consternation.

Here are some of the **states of emotion**, or feeling, that will ring some notes with you, to say the least. ** Notice some are *above the line* and some are *below the line* as I shall name them. **

I present these in a particular order here to describe a possible progression of your chakra activations, as the Earth society blunders through its present state of disintegration and decay of its present form.

However, notice that there is often no particular order of occurrence, and the notes of your emotions will jump around, often catching you off guard. Consider now, this *sequence of emotional states* which I will illustrate more clearly for you:

↑ **Vision, Enthusiasm, Inspiration coupled with Hope, Expectation & Hope, Reconstruction, Possibility, Opportunity, Relationship, Action, Togetherness, Feeling of Family, Satisfaction, Joy, Love, Comfort, Oneness, Sharing,**

Now, watch closely for the .... "CHANGE"

And, *inevitably*, how Societies are infiltrated with Greed, Entitlement, Separation, and Corruption … an inherent weakness in the un-evolved consciousness.

Then, notice how the STATUS QUO is tempting,

_____here is the line, the energy shift _____

↓ More Entitlement, Expectation, less Reality, Denial, Shock, Fear, more Denial, Sadness, Frustration, Hate, Disillusionment, Betrayal, Anger, Resistance (to the Change), Breakdown, Violence, Rebellion, Disorder, and *Revolution*.

Note that the emotional state of an individual and of Society governs the choices … that will be above or below the line. Look around you and observe your colleagues, and yourself, and the World around you … see if the shoe fits! What do you see? I ask you?

Can you see that when the two Divine assets of Love and Integrity prevail within, an Earth Being can move up the Divine ladder, I say once again, to meet and ultimately merge with the (your) Soul. This is your Soul Merge, folks!!

Alright. Do you know that a *Revolution* literally means a turn in different contexts? Your nations can experience these turning *cycles in the collective*, along with societies, groups, and certainly individuals.

> **I sponsor a "turning" in the present Earth consciousness that amounts to a revolution from the prevailing secular world mind set (now drastically infiltrated with rampant greed and often corruption with impunity, fueled by fear and thus by domination through the governing political and business classes) <u>into</u>** *a mind set of cosmic consciousness,* **embracing the vibration of White Light which flows with Love directly to and from the heart of GOD. This is the Cosmic realm in which I reside. I invite you to join Me in My lair!**

Again, I direct you to read and absorb your world's history books. You, in Humanity, choose the same *repetitive* cycles over your earth time, repeating the behavior over and over again. These cycles even precede Atlantis for goodness sake! When will Humanity evolve into the emotional states that allow White Light to become a *permanent installation?* You, as Light workers, are the ones We count on to lead the parade. More of you are required to step into influential stations of society and to then be able to prevail and this means establishing a critical mass of White Light. You must step up now! Know that *first* it is individual, then it expands to the *collective consciousness.*

So, here I AM addressing you individually at this point. That is where you and I start!

Did I not tell you that the *"same old tune"* will likely repeat? Here it is. Read these accurate Earth-world history books that I refer you to, ladies and gentlemen. Ask Me.

Consciousness, at this stage of Human development, is relegated to advance individual by individual, not as We in Spirit had *once* intended for the whole to roll over into the 5th Dimension of vibration in one heartbeat. This Divine maneuver of Spirit, in service of the Creator, was optimistically attempted upon Planet Earth, once your population reached a size of critical mass for this transmutation to be possible. In the Earth era of your years, circa 1960, most recently, this Blessing of opportunity was once again bestowed. And … the consciousness of Humanity was not ready and capable of receiving the Blessing, due to the very subjects of My transmission here!

Nota Bene, stripes are now figuratively sewn onto the individual Light worker's sleeves stripe by stripe, per Mastered initiation after initiation, and there is no free lunch. Dedication, perseverance, faith, and obedience are keynotes, along with a willing surrender to be taught by Myself and My Ascended Master colleagues, who will, if you choose to be willing, infuse you with wisdom, Love, and Blessings you can not imagine.

** See My previous transmissions addressing the *individual Light worker's responsibility for moving your consciousness forward.* We in Spirit can lovingly coach, guide, assist, and nurture you in your process, but We can not and will not make your Free-will choices for you. This is your lifetime. Ascended Masters have completed their turns around the Karmic Wheel of Earth. This is your time and the Earth window is not scheduled to stay open for an evermore, repetitious stream of lifetimes for you to rise up, "get it" and join Us in the White Light of cosmic consciousness above. The cosmic clock is ticking, good Ones. **

Alright. Once a Divine partnership is birthed, <u>you will be on your way to a new life beyond your current thinking, beyond your current belief system, and transcending the ordinary unexamined life so common in your secular world.</u>

You truly are the Light of the Heart, shining in the darkness of Being. So be it.

Now, more about CHANGE and how it affects you.

> **When massive Change confronts you, or a Nation, or your now more *integrated Earth plane, emotion plays a massive role in the outcome.* Master your emotions, and you can become a Blessed Spiritual observer of your current world events. You can become a part of the solution in alignment with Spirit *and thereby cease perpetuating unaligned outcomes.***

Fail to Master your emotional repertoire and you remain as a reactive energy force, caught in the continuing wheel of an enslaved behavior, the likes of which I have just described. Here you remain part of the collective problem, one of the billions of Earth-egos living in separation from Divine and Universal Law! It is called "being stuck" folks! We in Spirit wonder how many more thousands of years it will take for you to break through? The choice Is yours!

> So, when massive CHANGE presents itself, the art of DAILY BALANCING AND REBALANCING yourselves becomes massively important. It is available to you from within your Self. Balancing daily is essential for all Lightworkers now. The assignment is to transform your various emotions into the energy of Light, the energy of your Christ body. Your meditations and yoga balancing exercises are infinitely effective, as I have recently demonstrated to some of you. This daily practice is to become a part of all Lightworkers' morning routine, commencing now. You will thank Me shortly in your own way!

Fear is primarily the root chakra emotion blockage that will require considerable attention, and that is not to neglect the other six. This continuous balancing of your chakras will assist and enable the transforming of your fear emotions into the higher vibration octave of light. Your singing bowl *meditation* events are a pleasant way to purify, realign, and open your chakras. Take full advantage!

> As you RECOGNIZE your emotions and consciously focus upon each one as it occurs, you are halfway there. The second part is to *release your ATTACHMENT* to this emotion. And then to transform any negative emotional state into that of simply a Spiritual Observer or higher. See My book "Flight of the Soul".
>
> Find out what the pay-off is for your attachment. This will be up to you. Suffering is a too often outcome of your attachment.
>
> I believe in short suffering, folks!

Consciously allowing healing vibrations to encircle your physical body, and positively impacting your 7 lower chakras, is most achievable. Vibrations from your singing bowls, your herbal aroma oils, the human voice sounded in harmony, and certain musical instrument vibrations can all assist you in essential daily balancing. I now, however, will reveal something new to most of you!

Reaching out further, I advise you to seek out and practice daily the use of certain specific **Tai Chi hand positions and movements**, which can empower you to sense the energies present in each of your chakras at any given moment in time. These energies can be sensed, felt, and intuited simultaneously on a physical and mental level, for those with *developed sensitivity* and connection with their own "integrated circuitry", as you would describe it. *Once your technique is learned and Mastered, this process is most enjoyable and enlightening for Chelas, as the experience unveils the mystery of ever present emotions, perhaps otherwise inaccessible, locked away from your grasp.*

Here is a purified dose of *Practical Spirituality* for you to use daily! Let Us call it **Sliding Energy up the Spine**. While standing, with hands precisely configured in front of your chakras, palms slightly apart, *facing* each other almost touching (and not touching your body), very slowly move your hands together in unison (correctly positioned) up and down your *spine* and directly in front of all 7 of your energy fields, one by one. Hand movements are synchronized with your breathing at each chakra position. Take 2 or 3 breaths or more as your hands are in front of each chakra, and then slowly move this ENERGY UP THE SPINE, pausing in each position, beginning with the root chakra and ending with the crown chakra, releasing the final energy into the light! Slide the chakra energies up the spine and back down and then up again to fully feel the *sensation shift*, as your hands move in unison. The objective is to raise your vibration to the crown.

With concentration and practice, you will sense the distinct and unique *energy present in each chakra center, connecting you on a deep, perhaps surrendered Soul level, to the visceral feeling flowing in that chakra* at that moment. *Feel the connection with your Soul, sweet Ones.*

Empowered with this technique and the knowing it brings to you, you are then able to proceed, on your own, with an enlightened processing *of your sensed emotion(s)*. If One particular chakra is "shouting at you" there is energy there that warrants your love and attention. So, identify the current emotion that is triggering the chakra to be out of balance, and apply the principles I teach to rebalance.

Frequently repeat this "**sliding energy process**" and check your progress. With practice, you will be amazed with your results, and make this advanced process part of your daily morning yoga routine, good Ones!

Be assured that great satisfaction and relief is able to come forth from this unveiling. *As evident throughout this Saint Germain Chronicles book of Enlightenment, I devote much of Spirit's energy to assisting you in realizing and beneficially processing Ego's behavior, more often than not, routed in your emotions.*

I urge all dedicated Chelas as well as readers of curiosity to seek out a demonstration of this healing technique from One of Our Spiritual Instruments, including Lah Rahn, through whom I now speak.

So, these pages with My energies enfolded, embrace part of your *Grand Process*. This is not an academic treatise for you to find "interesting" or to memorize for recital at your next Spiritual gathering or cocktail party to impress the group with the vastness of your "Ego knowledge".

Your *Emotions in the White Light,* in the present moment, are part of your individual reality, in each moment, in the now. Now is Now. The next moment, however, can be re-chosen by you. It *can* include those emotions I call **above the line,** *which will empower you!* Do you remember the ↑ *up group earlier?*

Be conscious of the elements that make up White Light. It is a majestic combination of all the colors corresponding to each of the lower 7 chakras.

When combined in purity, these frequencies form White Light which resides in the 7th chakra of the crown at the top of the Human head. This light swirls round and glows as your crown chakra is in action, functioning as an Earthly extension of Holy Spirit energy.

Can you see this miraculous integration within the Human form? Please act in these times to include yourself in the magnificent group of Light carriers, that We may lovingly source your individual, unique Dharma in its purest form. Some of you will know that the Will of God is in action as you carry out My instructions … and your crown chakra will, as you say, "kick in" to function in Divine Alignment. When this dawning occurs, you will have an access to Spirit as never before. This is a promise!

The Blessing We promise is a new communing with the Holy Spirit far beyond your wildest imagination when your crown chakra, swirling with white light, connects your Being with pure Cosmic Consciousness. This is a reality We trust will encircle your consciousness in this Human lifetime! Yes, I AM speaking of Enlightenment! This is the realm of which We in Ascended Spirit are Masters.

AS YOU AND YOUR FELLOW LIGHT CARRIERS MASTER THIS *"SCALE OF EMOTIONS"* PROCESS, YOU BECOME MORE AND MORE "ELIGIBLE" TO REACH A HIGHER FREQUENCY OCTAVE, THAT OF WHITE LIGHT.

In this process, some of you may notice a ringing in your ears as your frequency elevates. And some may notice ringing only as a sign of aging. Can you distinguish?

Alright, … let this Transmission be your lesson for now. When each of you has put this writing, as a *Capsule of Wisdom*, fully into practice day by day, moment by moment, you may report back to Me for acknowledgement, nurturing of joy, and, of course, your next lesson of Light.

Be well and be obedient to access the gifts of which I speak. Those dedicated in Spirit shall rise above, while the *lazy and off course wanderers* shall be given only the just rewards of a status quo which evolves not!

A plate of plenty awaits those of faith. We bring signs of Our presence to you along with clues on a continuing basis. By all means, do avail yourself of Our Blessings through your restfully alert emotional management.

The consciousness of this Universe is constantly growing, changing, and evolving, and your shining evolution is a part of the miracle.

Be a part of the finest essence of Human life by taking the initiative to include all of your Beloved Self with your chakras in tow! Remember, hope is only the worthy companion of *action,* My friends. What is your next action?"

In Love and Truth,

Saint Germain

Through Lah Rahn Ananda

Listen and Talk to your Chakras

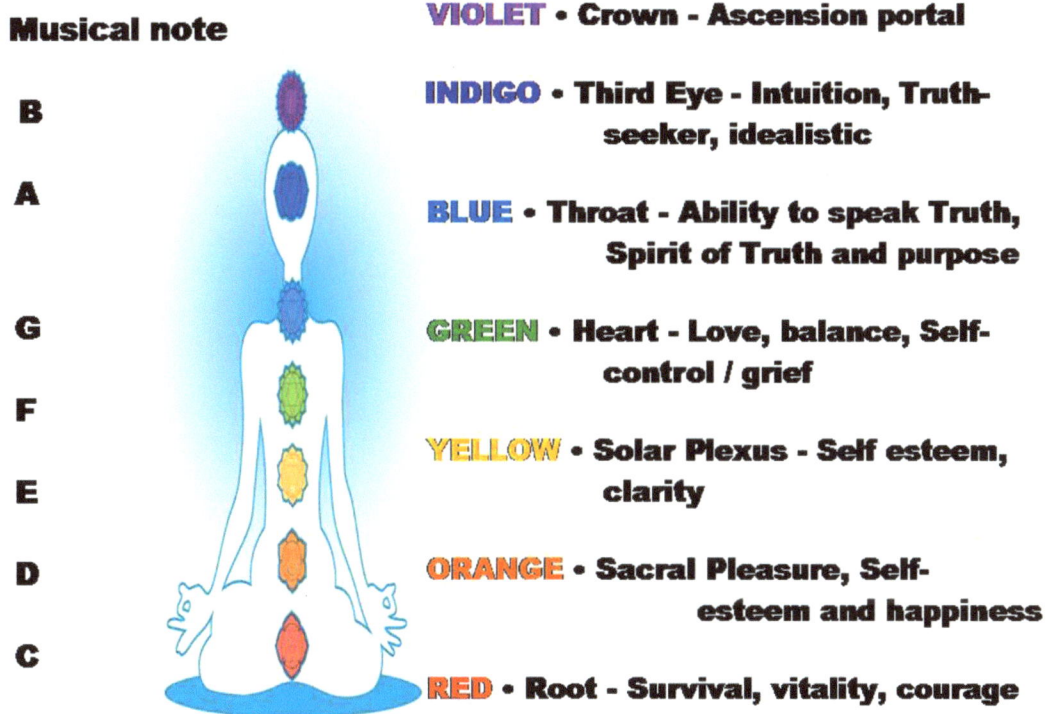

Musical note

- B — **VIOLET** • Crown - Ascension portal
- B — **INDIGO** • Third Eye - Intuition, Truth-seeker, idealistic
- A — **BLUE** • Throat - Ability to speak Truth, Spirit of Truth and purpose
- G — **GREEN** • Heart - Love, balance, Self-control / grief
- F
- E — **YELLOW** • Solar Plexus - Self esteem, clarity
- D — **ORANGE** • Sacral Pleasure, Self-esteem and happiness
- C — **RED** • Root - Survival, vitality, courage

    The chakras, or main energy centers of your body, are interconnecting spiral-chakras that hold physical, mental, emotional and Spiritual energy for you. These centers of energy react to life experiences as they affect you, voluntarily or involuntarily. So when you consciously make life's choices in alignment with Divine and Universal Law, your chakras react to *this conscious* input from a trained and purified mind, **mirroring how you have chosen to act or react to life as it unfolds.**

    Now, you are able to govern the frequency of your vibration. How did Master Sananda Kumara process and transmit input to his body chakras **to demonstrate Love** as he did? It was through **his conscious choice!** On the contrary, however, a choice to be fearful, angry or violent, … activates these corresponding lower body chakras. Remember though, **you can catch yourself** and re-choose in an instant when you are sufficiently trained, and your alternate choice in the same situation could then usher you into the upper body chakra vibrations.

    There is the Magic. Now you are a candidate to reach for and **hold the Divine White Light** that allows you *to transcend the duality of your secular world*. Only a cleansed and purified EGO need apply for admission here. So to assist you, that is why We in the Ascended Realm, recommend and insist upon **your daily practice of Decreeing** to re-balance, re-seed, and implant into your consciousness the highest parts of the Positive Vibration Range.

© Copyright 2014 Gordon W. Corwin IL All rights reserved. Contact: Lah@SaintGermainChronicles.org

Saint Germain speaks about
Heartful Devotion
and

The Blessings of Synchronicity

nes often ask Me to explain the essence of synchronicity and how this miracle relates to a heightened level of devotion to The Holy Spirit.

In the beginning and in the final ending moments of a devoted Soul's journey into the arms of the Holy Spirit, there lives an almost indescribable hankering and insatiable urge to reach more deeply into the depths of the etheric realms and to be touched by the hand of God.

Sometimes this pursuit is born into Being early **on in a violet Human lifetime, and yet more often it emerges later with an explosive inner feeling, a knowing that this pursuit is now the chosen path to be followed.**

In the Ascended Realm, We clearly observe this choice in you to be an almost uncontrollable and involuntary attraction but, at the same time, strangely agreeable and mesmerizing, … infusing the Spiritual inquisitor or Devotee with an insatiable hunger.

This compulsion is then often escalated to a joyful, tireless and unstoppable journey to reach further into communion with the Holy Spirit, where a Soul's Highest and Grand-Self can truly be touched and in turn touch the heart of God. *"Mastery" of this journey grants unto a Heart filled with devotion a Blessed life also proportionately filled with abundant Grace.*

Ascended Masters, Archangels, Devoted Angelic Beings and Divas all serve as your Divine Hosts and catalysts of White Light energy, to escort you along your ascension path. We Ascended do faithfully serve as God's emissaries to this end. We strictly act in alignment with Universal and Divine law as your loving guides and coaches, affectionately embracing every aspect of your Spiritual evolution.

As <u>Devoted "Ones"</u> of Heart move into Our vibration and portal, We find you extremely vulnerable, humbly detached and surrendered in a quiet state of mind that fully embraces a selfless life, including Divine service. Here lives an ego-waning "Beingness" and a remarkable openness of heart. Such a place of consciousness is where true healing begins. We notice that *Tears of Joy* will often flood forth from Our Devoted Ones, these tears appearing as one of your own Self-healing partners in this *phase of personal change.*

And for those of you who do not yet share in this lifelong journey into the seemingly mysterious unknowns of Spirit, beware that you too can, at any time, commence your surrender, growth, and consequent eligibility to be embraced by Spirit in unexplained and wondrous ways.

To underscore the birth of a newly-born Self, **We** in the Masterful Spirit Realm are granted the privilege of showering "Taken Ones" in the grandest of celebrations with Divine gifts, among which dwells the **Embrace of Synchronicity.** Perhaps you have experienced this gift?

If you have yet to experience the embrace of this gift, look around you for those who do experience these moments. Believe Me, these Ones are becoming more plentiful in numbers, as they willingly carry and radiate *Light* into your **duality of both light** *and* dark upon your plane.

> *This Divine embrace I speak of surely abounds,* **when a trained and grateful "taken" One, now awakened from a deep sleep, is imbued with an ongoing awareness and knowingness about Spirit, allowing discoveries of Truth to eventually overcome their shrunken Ego. Once experienced, Our embrace is unmistakably indelible and almost immeasurably uplifting. Ask a Chela!**

I tell you truly, Synchronicity is the delivery of Grace from the hands of Spirit, as God's emissaries. We, in the Realm, are imbued with the privilege and the power to make this dispensation to worthy Ones under Our care. Although We are unable to fill an Ego's cup that is already filled with its own arrogance, *We can bountifully Grace surrendered and "taken" Ones* with inconceivable joys, experiences, comforts, palatable life's lessons, and enlightened perceptions, gained only through achieved higher vibrations within.

Among these Blessings I speak of is a pathway pointed toward a fulfilled lifetime of self-discovery. Ingrained in the very fabric of a rising consciousness of enlightenment, is a process which may shock you here. But I shall proceed nonetheless. Teacher and student take their places! Let Me simply say to you that an incarnated Soul, *in the process of being "taken"*, perhaps at an early Human age or not, is **Gifted with the Opportunity to be Born Twice in a single lifetime!**

Your *first birth* is a biological gift granted to your Soul by Holy Spirit during your reincarnation process returning to Earth as an embodied newborn. Some Souls receive only the *first birth*, and then stop in their tracks, for that lifetime's incarnation! They are stuck in the mud! Their consciousness and free-will are in agreement to tightly clutch *Status Quo!* After all, change is confrontive by nature, for most.

Others, however, move into their *second birth,* as their free-will allows, developing a gradual Soul expansion through Blessings of Grace from Holy Spirit. It's Divine metamorphosis. I speak the truth!

The *second birth,* your rebirth, may occur, I say *may occur,* after your mind, body, and **Soul-Being is awakened from that initial deep sleep,** often after a *fall*. Your rebirth often involves your discovery of GOD and Spirit, tied to an embedded knowing from within, subconscious though it may be, that you are somehow engaged, and immersed in your process of gathering together all the shattered and broken pieces … often emotional and physical … from your fall, and miraculously placing "Humpty Dumpty" back, upright, once again sitting tall on the wall. Your Christ consciousness within, buried deeply as it may be, is now awakened, alive, and ready to begin the healing, a rebirth lifetime cycle … a reconstruction from within, We could say, sourced by your *partnership with Spirit, Divinely anchored in your free-will.*

Now, with this fresh foundation, re-integrated Ones are positioned to *recognize the higher dimensions of vibration,* and to walk hand in hand with Spirit, in some level of partnership along the path of their Dharma. Do you see Divine Alchemy at hand? We observe this regularly! **Many of these Ones** trudge through their process, only realizing they have engaged, once they are well along in their engagement and healing process! A further awakening and synchronicity is being delivered! ***Rewards come to those who experience this "taken" state of Being,*** often occurring at unpredictable times, and in mysterious ways.

Synchronicities, they are called. We dispense Grace in different forms, showering the unexpected, placing the low hanging fruit within easy reach. **Aspiring Ones** are amazed, as uplifting manifestations take material shape before their very eyes, in the midst of convoluted and often tumultuous secular world situations and circumstances and illusions. I create Divine Magic in mysterious ways, folks, and never to divulge My trade secrets, as you must realize by now! I shall add, however: take fine notice of hawks, owls, and ravens, as I may embody.

Moreover, you must beware that Divine dispensation of synchronicities can, at times, ignore the demands of an untamed Ego! Nonetheless, outcomes that ensue will inevitably have a *Divine meaning for you in your life-stream.* Such outcomes are often called life's "lessons", *folks!* This may take you by surprise.

Also, I hasten to add that the timing of Our synchronous gifting rests in Our hands and is often incongruous with the Earthly, Self-centered schedule of your Ego's calendar. Does this surprise you? Surrendered Ones who know Us often marvel at perfectly synchronous timing of their life's events when viewed in retrospect. Many will confirm this.

> *I predict that in due course you too will **gratefully** thank **Me** in retrospect for synchronizing your life-stream with*
>
> **"Divine Time".**

It is paramount that you understand, as well as **"know"**, about the very nature of Synchronicity and its use ... which is highly discretionary, **as the Will of God in action**. Our Lord El Morya often bears a loving hand here.

Egos would like the power to <u>demand</u> Synchronicity and Grace at the snap of an Earthly finger ... to <u>command</u> that it show up, at your will!

It may disappoint a delusional and untamed Ego to know that this power is outside of your grasp! Shall I say, "above your pay grade".

Only Spirit dispenses this Grace. Some insist upon repeatedly making "out of alignment" requests and prayers to Ourselves and to GOD for countless of your Earth days, months, and years ... **but nonetheless dispensation of synchronicities depends upon Divine merit, My fine feathered friends. It is the Law. Merit is determined in various ways by the Realm of the Ascended Masters and Our Father, The Creator, Himself. Disappointment often befalls those ignorant of this Law.**

The real nature of this Grace is very different from you simply calling to Spirit for an audience, ... as Our presence ... **and We welcome you** to access Our presence and commune with Us as some of you do. You are encouraged to call to Us much more often than you do. And,

> *Now, concerning the subject of manifestation, I have addressed this in different forums.* Suffice it to say for now that this ability, **when Mastered,** <u>can actually be used, at will, for Divine purpose</u> by evolved Humans of extraordinary enlightenment of consciousness *and* <u>done while incarnated upon the Earth plane at this time!</u>

WE are always available to be with you. Most of you need assistance to converse with Us, and We have a number of Earth channels to serve you in this capacity for direct access to converse with Ourselves in Spirit.

I mention this level of evolvement as an encouragement to those readers and Chelas who aspire with an extraordinary level of surrender and perseverance to reach greater heights. In the meanwhile, let Us focus for *your* benefit upon the Grace at hand for you.

Ones tell us that Our embrace delivers a sense of peace and tranquility and sometimes a <u>conscious</u> euphoria, allowing more effortless harmonies and the apex of manifestation to follow, as I have aforementioned. Have you dreamed of such Blessings for yourself? They are possible for you. I speak the Truth. We are fully committed to the acceleration of your *Light Bodies,* Dear Friends.

Teaching you to recognize the gift of Our embrace as God's Will is a formidable task, indeed. Many, if not most of Our synchronicities directed unto you, go unrecognized, ignored or simply chalked up to an "accident of fate" and your benefit, or a life's lesson, soon forgotten.

This is because you are inexperienced! Well, My Fine Friends, this is part of the learning process. One day *"Taken Ones"* discover, much to their amazement, that these "unexplained and mysterious accidents" are anything but accidental! They are the very synchronicities of which I now speak!

As you begin to experience and recognize these pinnacle moments, it would be wise for you <u>to consciously acknowledge to yourself their arrival and then give immediate thanks to Ascended Spirit for the perk, gift or absolute miracle, if that be the case.</u>

We recognize gratefulness with grand appreciation! I say to you that your future blessings, and thus the quality of your future life, may depend upon it!

Alright. So now, I shall delve more deeply into the mystery of this *Divine magic,* portraying this next segment … further wrapped in a vibration that will caress your heart, if you dare to allow such a Divine intimacy to penetrate your Being. I pray that you will.

**n particular, I speak today of Grace, delivered to eligible Ones of surrender, faith, trust, and service to Spirit, … Ones in pursuit of the Truth, with an openness to *Change*.**

Recently, a student Chela of Mine asked Me during a private reading to *define the meaning of Synchronicities*.

He rightly believes that he is now starting to receive these inexplicable blessings. He is correct!

Here is my reply:

The Chela Question (as recorded):

Aaahhh … My question? … can you please, ah … Saint Germain, explain Synchronicities to me, … please?

**Y response (as recorded live on 07-22-2010):**

"*Ahhhhhhhh. Synchronicities. <u>One of My favorite subjects!</u>*

Synchronicity … is that Blessing … given from Spirit … that is showered down upon a deserving One on Earth … to bring about faith in Spirit … to bring about joy … to infuse Love … to invoke Harmony … to assist that One in achieving their intended outcome, which is in Alignment with Ourselves.

Synchronicity … is God's Grace in action.

Synchronicity … is dispensed by Myself, by Lord Jesus, by Lady Master Nada, by Lord El Morya, by Lord Buddha (and many other Ascended Beings) …. and upon occasion, by the Holy Father, Our Creator, Himself.

Synchronicity … when it is given and recognized by you … will give you that much needed pat on the back!

Synchronicity will embrace you … hold your face … and lovingly stroke your hair.

Synchronicity will open new doors for you … where this Grace is dispensed as Angel dust that softly falls on your hair … your bare skin … on your clothes … your hands … and your fingers.

I can only wrap Synchronicity in My finest glove … in the most beautiful colours … in the most magnificent garments … and in all of the unconditional Love … of the Realm of Ascended Holy Spirit. I would hope this answers all that you could ever want to know … about Synchronicity."

Chela: Yes.

Saint Germain: Very good. (the reading continues, and then at the end), I wish you good day.

Chela: Good day, Lord Saint Germain, thank you very much, again.

Saint Germain for all My Realm

Through Lah Rahn Ananda

"I have recently transmitted to Earth Beings the Gift of an enlightening book entitled <u>Flight of the Soul.</u> *Herein, is a considerable and exhaustive explanation of specific steps toward Mastery, which you can choose to take. Moreover, you can Gift yourself by reciting daily the following "Light for the Soul" Decree, which is appended here to touch and comfort you, and to raise your level of positive vibration wrapped in Love. Now is the time of your test. We wish you new and buoyant heights and smooth sailing through the waters of your adventures in this lifetime. Speak with Me often, as I AM forever in service of all Humanity.*

Be well, Be Love, and Be of good cheer."

LIGHT FOR THE SOUL

Ascended Master El Morya

Transmission
Through *Lah Rahn Ananda*

Prayer of Divine Moments

Lead me, oh my sweet Lord, to choose thy bounty forever, for I know it is my destiny. Let me now hear your inspirations' love that guides me to make the most from each of our moments together,

for I AM one with Thee.

As your child, I stand in awe of the Divined free-will gift bestowed upon me and entrusted into my care. Guide me to heartfully know Thy will as I carefully choose each of my new moments. My right choices shall be the walk of my Dharma that I demonstrate in full view of the ALL,

for I AM one with Thee.

May I forever embrace the lessons of my moments which I know embody my own choices. Grace me, Lord, with true perception of my every moment, though parts be bittersweet, as I may choose to perceive. Let me see that I AM blessed by all of my lessons,

for I AM one with Thee.

Oh give me the awakened remembrance of my own Divine Self that reveals the true identity of Me to me in your likeness,

for I AM one with YOU.

Let my will be Your will forever and forever, oh my sweet Lord. Guide the steps of my walk to be trustworthy in the eyes of ALL. I pray to ignite the violet flame in the altar of my heart within each one of my newly treasured and joyfully shared moments with Thee. I AM your inspired instrument of Divine heart that chooses in love our moments together,

for I AM so in love with YOU

Oh my sweet Lord, my CREATOR.

EL MORYA

Through Lah Rahn Ananda

Just for you 2001

Acknowledgement
Marius Michael George Finearts

The Saint Germain Chronicles
Fifth Edition 01-2010

Lord Saint Germain joins with Lord Hilarion
From the Ascended Realm

The MYSTERY OF CHANGE

IF, and we say if, the Universe(s) turn in the fashion of a polar shift change for the Earth, the nature of that fashion would be a ***drifting*** vs. a sudden shifting of the poles ... and nonetheless, a new degree of precession - axis wobble - would result. It is unclear now, as to what combination of events *may occur, if at all. The cosmic dynamics are ongoingly unfolding as you read My words.*

In the event such changes do occur, the onset will be a *very gradual process,* not an engulfing overnight change. Adjustment by this Universe would manifest, in this case, by intermittent and mysterious magnetic failures and yet perplexing recoveries of electronic, electro-mechanical devices, and any *other Earthly phenomenon that utilize energy fields.*

Beware, even at this juncture, that without conscious attention, your *Human energy fields* can shift into unpredictable and violent emotional patterns, even more so than the lamentable patterns we now observe in higher levels of your institutions of bank commerce, where greed and fear often ruthlessly rule and rock Governments and men in domination and subjugation of the masses. On a softer and more subtle note, there could also be unexplained lapses in Human memory or awareness, until a conscious adjustment is made *by the individual,* using tools I have transmitted in my new book, to swiftly **restore a condition of BEING restfully alert and blissful in the midst of Change.**

Equipped with Spiritual Armour I provide, you can quite handily regulate your emotions, raising levels into the (+) Zone of Vibration, aimed toward unconditional love. Read on and brace, my fine feathered aspirants, as a Spiritual journey through the waters and **tides of Change** is not always pleasant for the unamenable, weak or the lazy! Even for those of you that are evolved to some degree, **Change by its very nature is challenging, if not confrontive and often seemingly devastating, as you walk to Master the Human condition.** I count upon your full engagement in your Mastery of Change, **a centerpiece of your evolvement.**

Your automobiles, computers, and availability of electric power in certain regions of the Earth globe, more than in others, will be affected if such dynamics come about. This means, then, that the <u>Human energy fields</u> I speak of in My most recent book (**Flight of the Soul** through Lah Rahn Ananda in USA) would also be affected; *thus the essence of My book – I advise procurement!*

A constant awareness and monitoring-adjustment of each Human's energy field to accommodate whatever Changes may come your way as an incarnated Human … is wise and mandatory of Chelas and walking Masters alike. No rest for the lazy, here! Those unaware, in denial, and unprepared with their Spiritual Armour can be swept up into oblivion, subject to a series of massive *personal* tsunamis that sweep over and have their way with everything in their path. So it would pay you to take heed and listen up … And re-read my *Flight of the Soul* book ongoingly, **as you shall neither understand nor internalize Our Wisdom until the fifth or sixth reading, cover to cover. Nota bene. Call upon patience and gentleness with yourself!**

This need to re-read will surprise many an EGO that regards itself as extremely Spiritual, advanced, intelligent and accomplished in the Human evolvement process. Know that you cannot demand a higher vibration from the Universe. It will be awarded unto you as you **are deserving and capable** of withstanding a higher intensity. As you control your own process of shifting the magnetic poles of ***your own universe***, as thoughts and deeds from one polarity (-) to another polarity (+), *then you have positioned yourself to merge into the changing energies of **your (our) Greater Universe***. Such positioning is also Our Divine prayer for you *irrespective of the precession issue!* Do you see Now? GOD integrates all of His creations and energies. And likewise, Energy is infinitely conserved in tune with this Law.

I AM showing you how to integrate your body, mind and Soul into the ***greater energy plan.*** Being responsible for your own vibrational heightening then gives you the ***deserving*** *entry level to be integrated* into whatever changes of Earth's magnetics or pole rotations that *may* occur. YOU will, in other words, My fine Blessed students, be in the "right place at the right time" as you would say. YOU will own as yours a new *vibration that protects and honors* at the highest levels. **Such communion with the Holy Spirit can infuse you with love and comfort everlasting**. Take heed of this gift that is yours for the earning.

YOU have incarnated in this life and you now live where you have chosen to do so. Now, in a new vibrational state of BEING, you will physically be drawn to be into that optimum geographical location to suit your Dharma and Soul, *should a relocation be relevant to your path*. I know this question obsesses many minds.

A word of caution for eyes and minds that would confuse My transmission(s) embracing the **Divine energies of the Holy Spirit** with your earthly religions at this point. We encourage teachings that are, in fact, in alignment with Universal and Divine Law, as stepping stones of comfort and humility for those who would choose a religion at some point in their life's path. While your earthly religious teachings **may** embrace certain Divine and Universal Laws, be alert and know that many of your earthly religions also harbor divisive and arbitrary and self-serving principles deeply imbedded in certain religious fundamentals, placed there to perpetuate a collective agenda of domination, fear and entrapment into a religion with no Divine basis. Listen to your inner voices, My good people. **Your Soul recognizes and <u>knows truth when you have access to truth</u>!** Meditation and your Decrees will assist.

Alright, so you say "where does this leave me now"? It puts you on the "hot seat", as you say, to get busy with your conscious attention to your Tests and Lessons of which I speak. We have nothing more to add. It has been spoken.

You must understand that! Your Free-will is in charge here and it is completely up to your choosing, not OURS.

As iterated above, I have recently gifted you with a truly enlightening and lengthy **Flight of the Soul** dissertation book. This is your Ascension Training at this point in time.

Mastery of My gifts to your ***Being*** upon Earth, coupled with your ***Soul and the Mighty I AM presence,*** shall lead you to Heights beyond your present Chela's comprehension, and yet within your very grasp! I speak of your **full partnership** with Spirit!

<u>Here in this new book is My comprehensive and exhaustive explanation of **specific steps toward Mastery which you can choose to take.**</u>

As always, dedicated perseverance is your merit worthy companion, along with Myself and Lord Hilarion, in this preflight positioning of your consciousness in full harmony with the Ascended Masters of Spirit. Moreover, you can gift yourself by reciting daily the Decrees which are appended throughout this work, to comfort you as you raise up your level of positive vibration wrapped in love. <u>Now is the time of your test.</u>

We wish you new and buoyant heights and smooth sailing through the waters of your adventures in this lifetime. Speak with Me often, as I AM forever in service of all Humanity.

Be well, be Love, and be of good cheer.

Saint Germain

Through Lah Rahn Ananda 01/2010

Comte Saint Germain

Portrait by Nicolas Thomas, 1783 public domain

Saint Germain
Sacred Changes
and
Freedom

 come unto you this morn to hold your hands and to wrap my fingers, as violet healing energies, around your heart. You might say you are surrounded by Love! And indeed, you are ... by the Loving Energies of all the Ascended Realm of evolution serving the Earth plane and the Spirit of Mother Goddess Earth herself. We are always present to embrace those Divining One's seeking full evolution into light and Ascension. Were there not *some parts of you* open to Our love and gentle tendering, at this moment, as you read with Me, you would not be reading! And your *vulnerability* to face change squarely and courageously is recognized and known as courage in the Heavens above Earth, where I reside in My Lair. Realize that energies of Earth changes, and also changes for Humans, are being vastly accelerated in these times.

You are all being asked to process your illusions of seemingly dire circumstances, your emotions, and feelings at a more rapid pace to gain the needed lessons to be Mastered, the surrender to your own Highest Self, and to move along to be prepared for the next round. Know that your attachments to the status quo of unaligned behaviors and beliefs now only cause hardship and suffering. This behavior continues to manifest from your lower bodies in the form of willfulness, stubbornness, unkindness and arrogance in relationships with others, and with circumstances alike. So I ask you to be willing to endure the consequences of falling down **when needed**, along your path, and **then to get back up** to recover your equilibrium and to regain alignment with Spirit ... *all in shorter periods* of Earth-time than before. **Balance** then opens your portal to receive more and more light of healing to launch your true Self with FREEDOM in the Aquarian Age. We in the Ascended Masterful Realm, along with the Angelic Realm, are here to assist you. Take comfort that you are not alone in this ever-present initiation of change.

Many are confused now with these rapid change onsets. I urge all of you to give special attention now to the management of your mental processes, particularly those coupled with the emotional part of you, stemming from your lower body energies. **Recognize that your illusions play a significant role. So, now I offer you a summary of some** *truths which shall assist those Ones who aspire to that of which I speak.*

First: about Duality: you know that ***Resistance Opposes Surrender.*** Be conscious to this truth when you suffer, for suffering is your ***"red flag" warning that Divine alignment has escaped your grasp*** … and self-correction is needed … a fork in the road to travel, if you please. Look to see "what am I really resisting here."

Second: Trust in Spirit releases Doubt and Fear. These times require **change from the Status Quo** to its opposite, the **Status-Non-Quo.** So beware that change shall henceforth be the order of the day … ongoingly!

Third: The "**What Is**" acceptance opens up Divine Opportunity. Light gloriously enters here and overtakes the darkness of separated EGO consciousness, which viciously, voraciously, and persistently attacks the heart and Soul, leading to lamentable consequences, indeed, My fine feathered friends. So, take some advice from above and begin your Decrees, if you have not already begun this practice. Decrees are essential. They assist Us greatly. ***They assist you greatly!***

Fourth: … surrounding your lower bodies: Your full exploration of human experience under Universal Law demands some suffering in order *to restore the SELF through the Grace of Healing.* As you proceed onwards, the Mental, Physical, Emotional, and frozen Heart aspects in healing all need to become YOUR ALLIES as you transcend, **versus** the harbors of your suffering. They are part of your multi-dimensional nature. They are there for you to Master and to pave the roadway to your personal FREEDOM wrapped in Enlightenment! You must <u>embrace and love your</u>

<u>initiations</u>, this in order, to transcend the hold that life's lessons have upon you. This *"love My-lessons perspective"* when practiced, will relax the stranglehold!

Fifth: the upper chakras: The upper bodies (chakras 8,9,10,11, and 12) can function in Grace and Beloved unison with the surrendered alignment of the lower bodies: **Lasting vibrations of serenity, calmness, joy and peace are achieved when healing of the lower bodies is <u>complete</u> and <u>maintained.</u>**

Alright! A multi-dimensional Being is synchronously supported by the Laws of the Universe in this balanced state of JOY and PEACE, when alignment is *maintained.* This is your natural state, to BE joyous and *FREE, whether it be in your Personal Universe or beyond.*

ALCHEMY.

Divine purpose and a surrendered heart keep you *centered in the light,* my Beloved Ones, and that's where I want you to BE. Aquarian Age transfigurations of the collective do require your full participation, in all the Healing and mysterious and magical upliftment of which I have spoken. *Alchemy is threaded throughout this book* to get you up on your feet – once and for All!. I thank you deeply for your willingness to undertake these ultra-human transformations. They are gigantic, ... but remember ... *So are You.*

In love and violet light,

I AM Lord St. Germain
Through Lah Rahn Ananda July 18, 1998

Unity, Separation and The Truth

**REETINGS, My Dear Ones, from the Ascended Realm of Spirit. Once again, We urgently call your attention to the colors of change, lights and darks, that now squarely face Humanity, challenging the purity of your pivotal Free-will life's choices on a global and an individual basis. Here is "Unity, Separation and The Truth" for your Well-being, expanded insights, nuturing, and Soul growth … this reality revealing Edition of The Saint Germain Chronicles, August 2008.**

SE caution, My Good Ones, about in taking and *absorbing* words that individuals write, especially upon your Internet, words easily interpreted as the absolute truth and final authority, then perhaps integrated into one's own belief system!! As I encourage in your life's journey on Earth, throughout this transmission and My entire book to follow, you are wise to attend caringly to your own Personal Universe, … a delicate creation, dear to your Well-being.

I would further remind you of your *personal accountability* for words, concepts and pictures you would subsequently circulate about and repeat. Careful selection of your words may impact the energy that your fellow Beings may choose to embrace. This leads to My next point!

Integrity is of utmost importance <u>for those who would be included in the Sphere of TRUTH</u> and in the higher realms of vibration. In this Sphere, integrity must be enormously emphasized, now as always, as it will be in short supply while battling to survive in opposition to the dark Sphere's momentum in these times.

Wise will you be when you acutely recognize and distinguish <u>between The Truth as differentiated from *massive amounts* of misinformation that are now being circulated around your Globe.</u>

* **No arguments please.** *

Also, you would be wise to now pause with pen and paper in hand, to list the countless illusions that appear before your eyes and touch your ears on a daily basis. Do you recognize that certain illusions in your 3rd dimension of consciousness are deliberately contrived by your fellow man to dupe your perception of the *Truth?* It's often called manipulation and domination, commonly draped in illusionary garb connected with your money and material assets! And then, other distinctions of illusion simply show up as irony! In either case, a close examination of Human illusions is at hand for you and worthy of your while, Dear Ones, as you seek *Truth*.

Take, for example, the following Earthly photograph of a completely flat-surfaced walkway in a prominent European city:

In your quest for Mastery of Enlightenment, I suggest you cast a sharp eye on the illusion which appears in your reality and lingers about you on a daily basis. Alright! In the process of distinguishing *Truth from illusion*, many of you have questions about the current state of Earthly developments affecting your lives. So, let Me proceed.

A societal and Earth-world cleansing process will run deep, and yes, there will be hardship and suffering for some. There shall be a great contrast between beauty and horrific events. Eighteen month doomsday-like predictions sourced by your religious Earthly prophets are "over the line", however. Earth Cleansing will be a gradual vise-like action, choking off some of the things you are all accustomed to having and seeing and doing. Cleansing will entail an unraveling of some economies, banking and business systems, with outward contraction extending to distribution systems for necessities of transportation and food, and some other supplies. <u>The currency of the US will certainly survive, although weakened significantly.</u> I say the Euro *may* survive (in whole or in part), *<u>a likely possibility and not a certainty.</u>* Reasonable preparations with monetary reserves would be most prudent while cleansing adjustments fall into place. Remember your principle of diversification. Maintaining order in certain parts of your globe, US included, will be a significant challenge, with some urban regions being particularly flammable and explosive. Governmental upheavals across your globe are in the making. After this cleansing, *a rebuilding will occur in a new order ... all in good time.*

For Light carriers, balance, compassion, and love are to be in sharp focus and <u>daily</u> practice. Alchemy can be brought to situations with little effort from the *Light of the Masterfully dedicated*. Writings in these Chronicles will give you valuable insights into this adventure.

The *Reconstruction will commence when the <u>collective</u> global consciousness <u>chooses to make it so</u>* ... when you (collectively) have had "enough" of the chaos, corruption and behavior, misaligned with Universal and Divine Law, to reset a lasting structure of TRUTH in your world, including the reality of higher Dimensions contrasted with that of your Earthly secular Third-Dimensional (3-D) realities and belief systems. This realization will mark only the beginning of this choice of change. The necessary critical mass can then be gathered, to begin and indeed to accelerate, the Alchemy of healing to enter into higher vibrational frequencies of consciousness, such as the 5th Dimension and higher octaves. We, in Ascended Spirit, are figuratively holding Our breaths to witness this choice! Remember Atlantis?

The Truth

"Dig deeply for rewards of the truth

where Earthly illusion fades into the dusk,

and joys of freshly found freedoms

Become Yours forever."

Saint Germain /Lah Rahn Ananda 2004

Understand that the energies of GOD and Spirit are massive, dynamic, ever-changing forces that adjust according to a present instant, or moment, if you will, in space/time. There are and will be *rampant false prophecies*, and more to come, bantered about willy-nilly in these times. What you allow into your sacred consciousness <u>will determine many outcomes for all of you individually.</u>

Some of you are at a crossroads and could grasp at straws. So, do watch your step and concentrate on walking upon those planted cobblestones in your Soul-path as they are your foundation. Step carefully. Get back to the basics! Does that sound familiar?

"Living Life by Design" or **"Living Life by Default"**

Now, those that are <u>awake</u> and able to listen to Spirit will <u>acknowledge their own call to consciously shed their Ego parts that no longer serve. These willing Ones … include yourself if you choose … are called upon to just BE.</u> In every moment. Present! That's all there is. Say often your "Present Moment" DECREE given in this Chronicle. Speak it, good Ones, these are *your present moments!* Present *"Being"* separates Light Workers from the dark Sphere of the unguided or simply dark Humans, pulling apart what could be a loving and integrated WHOLE.

Your *present* opportunities abound beneath the veneer of Human illusion. Surely, you recognize the *past* as done and gone, … old scrambled eggs that cannot be re-scrambled from the originals, and old original tapes from long ago. Know that the future is coming toward you at rapid speed, as accelerating energies of the *future* yet to be gathered.

Dark, religious for the most part, doomsday prophecies, such as in 18 months of this writing, are Spiritually unfounded. Dark energies of these naysayers and alarmists are intended to perpetuate fear and discontent, as misinformation continues to reward their futile frenetic behavior. The future of Earth and the Universe will unfold as it does in accordance with Divine Law. Awake, Light-bearing Humans will adjust to CHANGE AS IT ARRIVES. The *restfully alert* will blend these energies into their Human lives with Ease and Grace.

The rest of you will struggle, kick, shout and scream, and some will possibly arrange *their own* willful exit from your planet, to repeat the incarnation process in a place now undetermined in locale. Concentrate on My guidance here. Surrendered completion in alignment with your Dharma is an integral part of your Soul Contract and Covenant with God and Spirit. You may be joyful in your 'process' if you choose.

So, I urge you to live your conscious life each day in the Sphere of TRUTH, enjoy each moment as it presents itself, and be *fully responsible* for your self, your joy, your health and your Well-being, and then contribute to the Well-being of others in your own sphere.

And do stop worrying about your importance. Your joyful aligned service of Spirit and your fellow man is important now. You of Light are a magnificent part of Our Earth's assemblage of collective consciousness, representing those who stand united, together in the company of Great Spirit to re-amalgamate the **Sphere of TRUTH and FREEDOM as the collective Whole.**

I have been preparing Divining Ones for CHANGE for many eons, and now is another Earth-time when the mettle of all of you will be tested! I AM always available in My Lair to converse and commune with you. My invitation is open.

I ask that you insure that you have Me finely tuned in upon your Heaven-sent "wireless" connection and not dialed into imposter(s) who would lead you astray with misinformation apart from

Unity, Truth, and the Birthright of your

Divine Connection.

In Love and Truth with My Blessings,

Saint Germain

Through Lah Rahn Ananda

DECREE

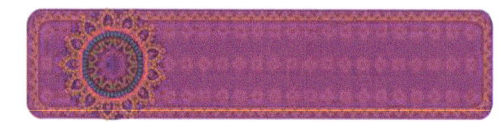

Present Moment

Once in each moment in present time
My Christed Self * I do align

In these my moments of reverie
Up spring the joys I choose to be

In times of care I see the Light

To violet I cling with all My might

Held in the Light, shining so bright
My glow is My call to shine on for all.

I AM God's Light shining so bright

To this I cling with all My might.

Repeat 3 times

* Many Ascended Deities Embody the Beloved Christ Consciousness: Krishna, Buddha, Jesus, Saint Germain, El Morya, Victory, Portia, Nada, Michael, Zadkiel, Chief Joseph, and many many more.

CIRCLES OF CONSCIOUSNESS

SEPARATION

THE WHOLE APPLE

A Collective CONSCIOUSNESS In Dis-integration

☺
Divine Law
Universal Law
Unity
Peace
Love
Co-operation
Win—Win
Harmony
Blessings
Grace
Abundance

TRUTH

Collective EGO BEHAVIOR Without Truth

☻
Ego always right
Domination
'Me First'
Subjugation
Abuse of Power
Greed
Conflict
Fear
Disorder
Combat ↓
Destruction

INDIVIDUALS CONNECTED TO SPIRIT
"Living Life by Design"

EGO-DOMINATED INDIVIDUALS
"Living Life by Default"

hich circle is knocking on your door?
Saint Germain

Through
Lah Rahn Ananda
10/20/08

OPENINGS for Opportunity

The Ascended Masters'
Library of Heavenly Wisdom

Channeled Works by Various Masters including

The Saint Germain Chronicles
Flight of the Soul Book
Decrees and Prayers
Illustrations
Masters Dissertations

Greetings to you all. This Chronicle Edition is dedicated to the long awaited introduction of The Ascended Masters'

Library of Heavenly Wisdom

WE, **as your enlightened and dedicated teachers from above,** commissioned by Our Creator to bring access of UNCONDITIONAL LOVE and pure LIGHT into your grasp, do now advise and remind you to make maximum use of the wealth of lovingly channeled and harmonized *gifts and teachings already given*. We observe a behavior pattern of your storing away and forgetting about the large cache of the priceless pearls which We have most generously and sumptuously showered down upon all of you Chelas for your enrichment.

Once received and read a couple of times, copious quantities of Our Divinely honed and carefully *refined Wisdom* are then put aside as "old hat", thereby downgraded in Ego importance or just ignored in favour of new works that an untamed, hungry Ego would anticipate as *fresh or more interesting than the old.* Nothing could be farther from the TRUTH ! **This Edition of the Saint Germain Chronicles** is dedicated to introducing the **Library of Heavenly Wisdom**, Ascended Masters' pearls delivered unto ALL of You in this Volume I, to merge with your consciousnesses, individual and collective.

It is no secret that in these Earth times of humongous change, you are in dire need for your own sake of *intaking and applying* Our wellspring of Wisdom and Blessings. I speak to you here on a personal level, and collectively as well, about your grand opportunities to polish and hone your Mastery of Human issues and emotions that would otherwise cause you to trip and fall. I speak here of your Human challenges rooted in fundamentals such as forgiveness, surrender to your *own* Soul, and downright greed. We judge not, as mistakes along the way are inevitable.

The *Blessing* is that the Ascended Realm of the Holy Spirit will pick you up when you fall, provided that you fully dedicate yourself to Our guidance, teachings and directives. Yes, folks, I AM speaking about that 110% effort on your part! And some, in their own process, are also unendingly devoted to serve GOD as a Spiritual observer, *as well* as a carrier of Light, radiating as a brilliant Chela. *When true surrendered devotion becomes your habit, what was effort then becomes joy,* My Dear Beloveds. Trust Me!

In due course, **as lessons are Mastered, lo and behold, you will begin to witness** your own evolution, unexplained synchronicities appearing as if by Magic (Spirit watches and showers Blessings from above, you know), and even admiration shows up from your co-workers recognizing a new radiance that hovers around your head and your new aura. **This** *is wonderful tangible progress, to be celebrated from above and below!!*

I, along with My Colleagues Ascended, unceasingly continue to nurture and support from the Highest your continuing dedication, perseverance, and surrender to reach the apex of your destiny.

Actually, you would be wise to calm *the Ego and think of your Earth consciousness doing its surrendering to your own Soul as your Highest-self.* In time, you will realize that this path indeed puts you in touch with surrendering to the Will of GOD, and your ultimate way of Being begins to evolve. Some of you do this automatically by now, … I AM most exuberantly pleased to announce. Others are enroute, shall I say, as your Ego-based consciousness is lovingly re-routed from its resident high ground!

Our Divine Library of Heavenly Wisdom contains ascension teachings and enlightenment guidelines which *will indeed shorten your Spiritual growth route,* saving you much unnecessary suffering and unneeded lost time *which is of the essence!*

So, now I turn to emphasizing the application of Our teachings at the *personal* **level,** where new **Openings for Possibility** are well within the grasp of many. (Refer to The Saint Germain Chronicles, My 2nd Ed. April 8, 2011).

I therefore issue this recommendation, admonishment, and directive to begin a campaign for Light Carriers … We rely upon you to re-focus and redistribute the voluminous works that have *already* been generously showered down upon you by Ourselves through the Light of the Soul Vortex. This process has extended through Our Instrument, *Lah Rahn Ananda,* over a period of 15 consecutive Earth years as I speak now, and continues further here as I speak. Remember, Our Wisdom is timeless and endures, despite your EGO's collective, impatient cries for "the latest news" from the Heavens! Opportunities are now at hand! So lend your hand!

As you receive Our channeled writings by various Masters, the Chronicle Editions, and My book(s), it would behoove you to set up your own organized, personal data base. We highly advise this action for your own reference and *also to assist your brothers and sisters who are in need of distribution from your own library that we provide.*

Your dedicated Founder, along with the devoted Pillars of Our *Light of the Soul Foundation* (of which yours truly is the Founding Ascended Master), ALL stand together, ready to answer your call for access to the Ascended Masters' **"Library of Heavenly Wisdom"** now available to you. We offer this collection of works at negligible cost to your Earthly pocketbook, save a miniscule effort on your part to ask and receive. Here is your opportunity.

Teachings to transcend and Master your many Earth lessons are beckoning and at your fingertips for the asking. For the sake of your Soul's evolvement, I implore you to rise to the occasion, treat yourself to new visions and paths of *less "doing it on your own hardships",* and to seize the day! Remember, *Chi la dura la vince.*

It would be wise to get your acts together folks, as *your life's play* is already *in progress. The curtain is up!* Each of you, My Dear Beloveds, will inevitably have your final curtain in the *Divine Order of All Things. My Dear Beloveds,* your finite time clock is ticking, during which time you can choose to evolve and to Masterfully shift and perfect your consciousness! Old Earth sayings speak: Time nor tide waits for no man, and Carpe Diem.

You have chosen to lead and pursue an *examined life*, a life worth living as your Socrates taught centuries ago in your history. So step up and receive every Blessing available to you! I say to you that discipline and perseverance is now being *put to the test*. I pray you pass muster and step up to give yourself a passing grade!

The Grand Process

"LEFT AND RIGHT *TOGETHER*,

JOIN

THE ABSOLUTE AND THE RELATIVE.

REALIZED WITHIN MY BELOVED BEING,

THIS INTERNAL CONJUNCTION

BEGINS

THE MIRACULOUS BIRTH OF MY

ENLIGHTENMENT"

Blessings,
Lah Rahn Ananda 2013

You are all eligible to receive copious dividends by heeding Our words, if you will only follow Our directives. Focus you must, from this moment forward, your keen attention upon *integrating the pieces of your own karmic puzzle.* As an actor upon the stage of Human Life, you are presently in the *spotlight and learning to shine as the sun from within.* And now, you must learn your lines. By heart ... and by mind if you must. We, as Ascended Beings on behalf of the Creator, are part of your audience along with your Soul. Your fellow brothers and sisters are also part of your audience ready to witness your transformation and **victories.**

Alright, My fine feathered friends, these are your marching orders. We are here 24 x 7, as you would say, to love you, to nurture your Being, and to guide you. Talk with Us whenever you wish. And, always remember, that it is *you, not Ourselves, who make choices and you who take steps.*

> **The steps you choose mark imprints in the sands of your Soul. Step with care, Dear Beloveds.**

I urge you to embrace and apply on a daily basis,
The Ascended Masters' Heavenly Library teachings
and Step into your Cosmic Consciousness.

You were born to shine! This is your hour!

Saint Germain

Through Lah Rahn Ananda 04-22-11

More on
The Ascended Masters' Library of Heavenly Wisdom

Here, you have at your fingertips an easy access to original, contemporary Spiritual Channelings from a number of different Ascended Masters of the Holy Spirit. United, We are fully aligned in Love and We devotedly represent the Creator of this Universe.

This priceless collection of **Heavenly Wisdom Dictations** has been amassed over the past 15 years under My direction, as Saint Germain. The Library continues to dynamically expand as new energies from Holy Spirit are transmitted to Earth in the form of *practical Spirituality*. My individual dissertations, The <u>Flight of the Soul</u> book, The <u>Saint Germain Chronicles</u> book, Prayers, Decrees, and striking Graphic Illustrations are available to you.

These nurturing and instructive Blessings serve as a gift to Humanity, assisting to rebirth Mankind's everlasting opportunities in raising your individual and collective vibrations into the higher ranges of violet and white Light. The united voices in this Ascended Masters' collection are harmonically blended and focused as a single beam of Light intended to unite with *your Soul's mission* to *transcend much, if not all, of the Human condition as the end objective of this incarnation. Ascension and its requirements, embodied or out of body, are unceasingly addressed for you throughout these transmissions.*

<u>Your dedicated application and integration</u> of Wisdom in this Library <u>into your every day life</u> is infinitely important, dare I say essential, to the evolution of your consciousness in order to prepare for and to enter into *Ascension Training,* which is the subject of my recent book, "<u>Flight of the Soul</u>", in this Library.

Kindly be well and of good cheer as you walk along and traverse your Spiritual journey. I AM unconditionally committed to Our Divine partnership and to sourcing your walk with all of the Light the Heavens can muster for your *ultimate victory* with My Blessings.

Saint Germain and El Morya and the Realm

Through Lah Rahn Ananda 04-22-11

The Holy Presence

I AM that I AM
I AM that I AM
Oh GOD I know that I AM that I AM.

I AM I AM Beholding ALL
Mine Eye is single as I Call
Oh Raise Me Now and Set Me Free
Thy Holy Presence Now to BE.

Repeat 3 times, ending with

Om (A-u-m) mmmmmmmmmmmmm.

The Sacred sound of Om is here to assist you in effortlessly melding this Decree with your body, your consciousness and the pulse of GOD's Universes.

Freely breath in and exhale the essence of these words in your own rhythm, tuning your voice and breath to merge yourself with the Eye of GOD. Seeing near and afar with your third eye will render your consciousness into an amazing proximity with the *enlightened perspective abilities* We wish for you. Receive the Blessing in Love.

Following this Decree as you begin your meditation, allow your mantra to drift your mind into a conscious silence of daily rest and healing. Daily *practice* I ask.

I AM with you always and pray for your alignment with the Will of God which I hold and anchor for Mankind in My Blue Ray, the First Ray of the Holy Spirit.

El Morya through Lah Rahn Ananda

Ascended Masters
Saint Germain and El Morya

GOD's Business and Your Free-Will

ELCOME WORKERS OF LIGHT.

Master El Morya of Holy Spirit's First Ray, embodying the Will of GOD, joins with Me this day to spread Our energies over Humanity and Planet Earth to bring Enlightenment.

As Saint Germain, CHOHAN of the Aquarian Age, together with My devoted Ascended colleague El Morya, *We* bring you warm greetings from Our Realm on high. Together, *We* shall speak this day of your Free-will, Soul Contract Vows, Cosmic and Human matters, surrender, Divine rewards, and the Will of GOD at the pinnacle.

Many of Us in the Ascended Realm find that *We* are currently being quoted via your UTube.com and other Earthly media. And further, *We* observe that **certain of these transmissions** are brief and need expansion or clarification. Master Lord El Morya and I are here now to provide this service to all Humanity through this 8th Edition of the Saint Germain Chronicles.

When you see and hear mixed messages that sparsely touch many topics, and you are confused, ... you are not alone in your confusion. Your Brothers and Sisters join you frequently. So, *We* will sort out certain issues for you here, and in true fashion, Dear Ones. *We* will speak Truths that need to be spoken and re-spoken now in these striking times of your Earth changes.

Yes, your Ascension work and process can continue with assurance in the face of Earth changes as they come about. New lessons from these changes will act to enrich your training, contrary to the comfort of your EGO and mind, which constantly seeks to have it ALL the EGO's way. Those Ones of you in harmony with the Will of GOD are placing their energies on their SURRENDER TO GOD's WILL AS IT UNFOLDS AND NOT UPON FEAR-BASED SPECULATION ABOUT WHAT GOD'S WILL SHALL BE! Our suggestion is that "Worried Light Workers" get their priorities in order! Read on, My good Fellows and Ladies!

On a smaller scale, yes, Mankind has collectively learned how to forecast certain Earthly phenomena such as weather patterns, tornados, rainstorms, floods and at times, certain astrological influences of your Solar System's Planetary array. We Bless the accurate prediction of such *events* in advance of their arrival. Human life and well-being can indeed often be enhanced with proper action. Note however, that Man has not been quite so successful in predicting the quakes and shakes, and shiftings of the mantle of Mother Goddess Earth! Have you wondered why?

On the Grand Cosmic Scale, the Will of GOD Is, and Is what it shall Be. It is dynamic in nature, and cannot be prophesied!

Divine energies are continuously evolving and will BE as they will BE.

Reacting in fear to predictions of Cosmic events by Earthly Gurus is not your calling nor concern, ... as a SURRENDERED BEING.

Cosmic events are Mother-Father GOD's business! Know that these events on Earth are integrated with Spirit's awareness. You and your Brothers and Sisters can trust in the **Divine process**. So, relax, observe, adapt, act, and readapt as you need.

As to your individual energies, you would be very wise to place your attention upon carrying out your *individual Soul's contract,* pursuing a motivated and inspired lifetime of extraordinary self-discovery and Mastery ... in place of emphasizing these fears of EGO that often take top priority and squander your precious energy.

There is an answer. Do you know your answer? You need to choose very wisely in these Earth-times of great Change in order *to perform and Master your Soul contract's assignments and missions. We* say, ponder these questions in your quiet moments. Ask Me, and I will reveal this answer.

> **SEPARATION of your consciousness from the Will of GOD** and the ALL of ALL requires a gargantuan ransom to be paid, ultimately sacrificing your Ascension. If you choose, you can continue to feed your *fears* that your mind and Ego would want to promote. **This choice is yours.** You can also choose to feed *your own sweet heart of love and the nurturing trust* that your Soul beckons!

White Light is a Blessed energy used miraculously by the Angelic Realm, the Divas, and the Divine Ascended Masters to protect you, to soothe you, and to *elevate your consciousness, as Cosmic events unfold*. So, open your heart chakra and allow this Light to embrace your Soul. Take a moment. **This is your invitation!**

Indirectly, you have all been asking about the "protection" you can expect from the Holy Spirit. The short answer is that Spirit's protection is dispensed in *direct proportion to the degree of surrender your EGO has achieved combined with your devotion to Universal and Divine Law. We* are simply speaking here of your alignment with Spirit, and Blessed synchronicities that can follow, My good Ones!

Again, it is your choice either to be on your own, in separation, and to have it your **EGO's way ... Or,** a choice to be joined and connected with Us by asking for, listening for, receiving, and acting upon Spirit's Divine Guidance. **The Divine voice, ...** Our words, images, information, ideas, and intuitions and much more, may come unto you directly or as spoken and written through one of Our chosen channeling Instruments, … such as demonstrated in this very transmission you read now, … once you have chosen to be sufficiently surrendered to be spoken to! For your absorption, Re-read these lines, if you would, please.

So, in this listening process *We* describe, you *begin or continue* to blend your consciousness with Spirit, such that ultimately they are ONE. *We* surely have fully trained, living and walking Masters upon your plane, that demonstrate this capability ongoingly, although admittedly, few in numbers at this time. *We* assure you all that this feat of Mastery to access the Divine Mind is most possible. You may ***choose to be chosen also, in good time, as continuing initiations of life strike your Being and Mastery becomes your vibration,*** My Sweet Chelas.

Please trust that *We* continue to call and summon the Angelic Kingdom on your behalf to work tirelessly under Our supervision, *particularly in the Sacred deliveries of Blessings of Grace.* Our energies are in concert with **Archangel Michael and Archangel Zadkiel**, who lovingly continue to answer Our call, legion after legion. Does this explain why some of you are now beholding gentle Angelic forms floating around your bed as you lay down your head to rest? Can you identify any of them by name?

As part of your process of devotion and surrender, Blessings will open up for you and higher vibrations will expand within your auric field. You will notice increasing numbers of synchronicities and Blessings of Grace arriving in your life, providing indescribably magnificent sources of joy. Many of you have sampled the sweet nectar of which *We* speak. You can expect to experience a mystical sense of inner peace and euphoria if you continue to apply the dedication your Soul requests, … and then to apply Spirit's constant course corrections to your thoughts, emotions and actions. Again,

We say certain of Our devoted Instruments of Spirit can source you by speaking Our words directly to you as We dynamically speak to you in real-space-time through the Instrument. In short, this is known as the channeling of Spirit! Our Instruments are finely attuned to *Our* vibrations, and dedicate their lives to serving Spirit and Divining Souls, sailing their way along to surrender into Oneness with GOD.

Alright. At this juncture, We must make clarification surrounding the subject of <u>Human Free-will and its aligned use.</u> Upon Planet Earth, Mankind has been gifted with the use of *conscious and unconscious Free-will abilities, as an integral part of being Human.* We speak here about the <u>Earthly Doctrine of Free-will, implanted in Humans by the Will of GOD.</u> In this regard, Mankind is a major Cosmic experiment to find out if Humanity can evolve into use of its Free-will, <u>aligned for good,</u> and <u>simultaneously restrain the negative uses spoken about in this transmission</u>. The test of this challenge is a miraculous gift from the Creator, and an *absolute focal point in the Ascension process.*

This Free-will gift to Humanity is in contrast to *certain* other star systems populated with Beings not yet fully evolved, and yet, possessing advanced technologies. These Beings are *not granted the gift of Free-will, despite their abounding technology*; also, many of these Beings are <u>ironically</u> *in separation from the Divine Realm, as We have spoken.* **Technological advancements ... e.g., "flying saucers" ... beyond your Earth science at this point ... often confuse** Humans as regards Divine connectedness. Know that certain other star system Beings <u>are fully evolved in the Divine sense</u>, and Our Pleiadian brothers and sisters present full evidence of this advanced state of consciousness. The Pleiades, often called the Seven Sisters, are a star cluster in the constellation of Taurus, which you would be wise to gaze upon! Take heart in knowing that these Beings demonstrate the next step for Humanity, depending greatly upon Humanity's future ability to master ego management and correct use of free-will in Divine alignment.

> Humanity's gift of <u>Free-will</u> is a <u>Blessing</u>,
> an <u>unavoidable responsibility</u>,
> and a mammoth lifelong test … all rolled into One!
> <u>Mastery</u> of this test ultimately joins
> an enlightened Human Being
> with the Will of GOD.

We shall now begin with the <u>Blessing</u>. Imbedded in Soul contracts, *We* find assignments and agreements made by re-incarnating Souls. Included are vows promising to re-discover Divine dimensions, as distinct from the 3rd Dimensional secular world; then to firmly and effectively grasp and Master the process of Spiritual purification by shedding layers of EGO skin; then to refine the purified consciousness, *thus aligning with the Will of GOD as One*.

Performance of these vows, all in one single lifetime is, indeed, a humongous assignment to undertake! *We recommend <u>you do just that</u>*!

If you were to regard this journey as super Human, We would not protest your viewpoint. Because, in fact, that is the courage you now show Us when you fully engage here and trust in your intuitive recognition of Truth!

This <u>Soul's mission of purification</u> is the heart of your Ascension process. Be aware, Good Ones, that this process continues for an entire Human lifetime and involves two (2) fundamental aspects.

<u>The First aspect is</u> to consciously learn and apply the *wise practice of using your* Free-will Gift from GOD. This assignment entails training to learn about alignment and then to *consciously apply your Free-will in that correct alignment* … moment by moment, day by day, … <u>all in spite of what your EGO may be saying to you or demanding as your ruler, when you start this process</u>. Spirit will make "suggestions" for you to follow.

Your test is to <u>willingly</u> comply with your Soul's calling. Later in your evolvement, this compliance will become a joy! … as difficult as it may seem to many of you now, <u>who are entirely out of your comfort zone</u>! The <u>transmutation</u> of *complaint into joyful compliance* has happened for many Chelas that *We* guide and direct. Join in with Our cadre of aspirants and partake of the joy!

Let *Us* further clarify, My Dear Ones … a refreshing revelation for most! In order to become a fully surrendered Being upon Earth, *you need not "Give Up" your Free-Will. We do not invade or violate Human Free-will.* You will not be forced by Spirit to become a "robot" carrying out dominating directions that you receive. Your test now, is in *how you use your gift !*

Mastering your use of Free-Will is in large part the quintessential ingredient of your Spiritual journey, folks. This is the "ball game", as you say. Aligned use of this capability then opens further doors into GOD's mansion, which otherwise can remain locked and bar your entry!!

Are you following Our dissertation here? Re-reading Our words will assist you. *We* strongly direct you to read and re-read and absorb this entire Edition at least five (5) times before proceeding to the next Chronicles Edition … to secure your foundation of understanding, transmuted into knowing!

What you must give up is letting your EGO make ill-use of your Free-Will! And after that, you must learn to <u>willingly</u> align your Free-will actions and decisions!! A tall order We acknowledge, and one you are capable of executing. The process entails many blunders and false starts initially, and then Blessings of success begin to show up. And sometimes, *We* will pick you up! *Believe Us, this becomes easier as you become more Masterful.*

<u>The Second aspect of your Ascension process</u> is to alter those negative <u>EGO characteristics</u> that clutch you in *separation's vise-like grip* … and then to replace these with <u>aligned and automatic characteristics</u>, behaviors, and traits such as Love, kindness, joy, sharing, harmony, giving, consideration, fairness, empowerment, honesty, win-win thoughts and actions, … in conformance to GOD's laws and (some parts of) Man's

laws, … excellence in honorable pursuit of your aligned life's actions, goals and career, and most of all, of a full engagement with the Holy Spirit as a Divining Partner.

Your *negative* EGO parts, on the other hand, are the separate parts of you that foster Separation from Truth! Don't worry, you are not alone here. Every Divining Human goes through the process of purifying and transmuting the EGO drivers that *We are about to enumerate. Note also, every Ascended Master has successfully Mastered and transmuted these EGO drivers and behaviors, now washed away, and discarded, released into the Light.* **Oneness** *is a favorite Mantra for Us as We float about in the Ethers.*

So, exactly what are some of these EGO Drivers, as *We* shall call them now? … these EGO traits that resist, ignore, or overlook a Soul's calling to discover and heed the Will of GOD? Beware, this is only a *short* list, folks.

Unyielding at first, an EGO exhibits traits and demands of hypocrisy, selfishness, boastfulness, 'me first', impatience, negativity, anger, revenge, hate, fighting, warfare, deceit, dishonesty, cruelty, greed, fear, arrogance, lying to get its way, cheating, thievery, falsification, acrimony, usurping others' Free-will, excessive dominance, corruption, disobedience of GOD's Laws, Universal Law, and Man's laws, obsessive attachments, over-indulgence, malice, gluttony, disregard of the Truth, twisting the Truth, being unaccountable and irresponsible, … and a boundless number of other EGO traits that can be neutralized and then transcended with your dedication and compassionate assistance from Ourselves.

Observe yourself as you review this short list. *We advise that you check those that apply and then weed your garden daily, if you want to traverse the road to Mastery, enlightenment, and Ascension here.*

To further assist you with your essential transmutation of negative EGO behavior into Your Highest-Self Choices, *We are* **including with this Edition an essential Addendum to** The Saint Germain Chronicles**, entitled** Tuning Up Your Vibrations. *We* **believe use of this gift will well serve your introspection and ongoing self-examination leading toward your excellence!**

Throughout a Human lifetime, an EGO unfailingly faces countless decisions requiring the use of Free-will to choose actions, thoughts and emotions. These can be aligned with Spirit, or centered upon "doing it the EGO's way", … your way. Many start and finish an entire incarnation in separation, *choosing their way, believing that* *they know better than GOD, only to repeat the process in subsequent incarnations.* In contrast, others take another path, but often after seeing the Light that their methods are not working! *Some* must often reach an Earth age of 50 years before concluding this realization! *Others see the Light* in childhood or in early adult years. Either way, many are open to changing their ways and to embracing the guidance of their Grand-Self, their Spirit Guide(s), or ideally, the guidance that they themselves can access *directly* from the Divine mind. This is a process folks, and it is undoubtedly the most *challenging changeover* you will make in your Earth lifetime!

Surrendering Ones have most often found that the "hills of life" are *too steep to climb alone, in separation*, and they gravitate into the White Light of Spirit to sustain life, or better yet, to enhance an evolving life. They have had enough of acting out the EGO's way! Many are drawn to Spirit through a force *they find Magical* and coincidental. <u>On the contrary</u>, Dear Friends, their Soul has opened up and *invited Spirit to come in*. This attraction is not an accident.

> As God's Representatives to Humankind upon Planet Earth, *We* act in full alignment with Divine Law and introduce Ourselves. Under Divine Law, Spirit will not violate, dominate, or over-ride *the Free-will of an individual*. We must have your consciousness permission to enter your space. We joyfully honor Law! This is Love!
> This is Freedom!

<u>***We* speak next about your responsibility**</u>. All of the above means that for an ***entire Earth lifetime***, you have the responsibility (joy or burden if you so wish) of choosing, moment by moment, how you use your gift of Free-will. Such an enormous assignment and responsibility, indeed!

Ah yes, ... now what is this *"Lifelong Test"* of which *We* speak?

A Divining Human Soul, carrying through their incarnation of their *"vows of Soul Contract",* will be unceasingly tested for the <u>worthiness of their choices</u> of Free-will. Some mistakes will be made and consequences born. Blessing and kudos will follow. *Aligned choices* will be devoid of EGO's unruly energy, that ignores Divine guidance. *We* have need not to elaborate here for you about EGO's drunkenness upon your abundant liquor. Ahem.

> **Again,** *We* **say those ushered into Our Sacred embrace are free to choose** *whether to stay or not,* **using their gift of Free-will in this process. IF they stay and pursue enlightenment and Truth, they will continue to use Free-will to make aligned choices as they walk the path** *onto greater Spiritual evolution and into Our arms.* **Spirit is a grateful witness to millions of Ones that have chosen to persevere and stay on the path. The numbers are now increasing exponentially.**

About your rewards. As a Soul steps upon each stone of its Dharma, traversing a narrower and narrower path toward Spirit and Oneness, there are Blessings dispensed that bring about euphoria, described by some as ***Divinely*** intoxicating. (Not as *your* liquor would pickle your thoughts and actions). But rather, a euphoric peace of mind, about your personal circumstances and Cosmic matters alike, will begin *to envelop your Being.*

This blissful intensity will increase and accelerate as One moves into a deeper surrender, coupled with Free-will service to others and to the Divine. Fears on many levels begin to fade away, along with judgments of others and judgments about Spirit as well. Synchronicities appear and then become more commonplace. Others will recognize your Light <u>without you telling them about it</u> ...Your humility would never allow such an indiscretion. Your hunger for recognition will fade, replaced by a satisfied inner feeling of joy, knowing how you have <u>chosen and re-chosen in alignment</u>, over and over again. *We,* in Spirit, will become more visible to your Third Eye.

Our presence will become your constant companion.

Do you know that *We* in the Ethers never sleep, and are in unending service to GOD and to each other in the Ascended and Angelic Realms? In time, certain Ones of you will be invited to briefly visit Us in Our Ascended Chambers. Our invitations are often tendered to you during your periods of restful or REM sleep, where *We* can access, with your permission, the deepest parts of your consciousness *for nurturing and purifying.* A most pleasant experience, indeed, as many of you already know!

With the greatest Love and most profound caring, *We* bring all these Blessings to deserving Souls who stand with Us in the Light. Can you not see what Grand Blessings lay ahead for you, when you make choices as *We* have spoken?

Many of you are now at a point to decide and choose to <u>awaken</u> and to embrace Spirit, thereby choosing to allow your Soul to be fed by the Light. OR, you can choose to be fed by the fears that are lingering in your mind and Ego, confused with untamed emotions that need to be cleansed for progress. Which path do you choose? When you finish this Edition, see Saint Germain Chronicles, 10th Edition, "Dealing With Your Fluctuating Emotions". The strings of your heart await healing!

Speaking to you only as Saint Germain, for a quark or even a gluon of Cosmic time here, My *"Flight of the Soul"* **book is intended to train and guide students of the Light in this Spiritual Ascension process.** As expected by the wise, it presents a formidable challenge by nature. You are advised to give attention to this wisdom, also waiting for you, waiting <u>at your very fingertips</u>!

So, while you ponder these confronting enigmas, *We* suggest you humbly become a <u>Spiritual Observer to Earthly and Cosmic events.</u>

This, my Dear One, is the Spiritual observer you are meant to be! … strictly an observer here, surrendered in faith and trust, to concentrate upon <u>***your own Ascension training process,***</u> without worry of things out of your control (<u>or "above your pay grade", as Earth-goers say</u>).

We *invite you to utilize the full power of the* Flight of the Soul *Ascension Training book, along with the many Editions of the* Saint Germain Chronicles, to open your heart chakra to love, without harboring those nagging fears, and free to now put your energies upon your personal Ascension assignments.

About the *Flight of the Soul*

Ascension Training Book

by Saint Germain

THIS IS ABOUT YOUR SPIRITUAL BUSINESS, Folks. You will be surprised at the assistance waiting for you in the <u>Flight of the Soul</u> book as you journey forward. In these emotionally charged Earth-times, you are now encouraged to <u>consciously stay in the Light,</u> and release your fears and negative emotions using the <u>techniques</u> that are outlined in this Flight of the Soul book, I have recently transmitted. It is focused upon making you ready for your Ascension.

Embraced here within is guidance for Self-management of emotions and how they all correspond to your energies held in the physical body chakras. You will need training to accomplish this feat. You will need to be guided by Ourselves and the Angelic Realm to concentrate upon those parts of your Spiritual journey which you can <u>learn to self-direct</u> and to Master, as a maturing Chela of the Light.

When you embrace the <u>*Flight of the Soul*</u>, **you shall have reached a critical turning point in your time of Awakening!** *Your Spiritual process and path await you.* <u>*"Only through tireless and devoted practice of your process will you break through into new territory of boundless and endless transmutations required for your ASCENSION."*</u>

Flight of the Soul, pp 11.

As **Saint Germain** and **El Morya**, *We* **Bless you with Our melded energies as ONE**. We offer you this guidance in the highest love and affection that *We* represent … The Divine Mind.

Can **We in the Ascended Realm** trust that you will <u>act upon Our guidance</u> and move forward in your personal process to Master the challenges that lay ahead in your Spiritual journey? Yes indeed, *We* do place Our trust in you, along with Our gratitude.

With Greatest Blessings of Love and White Light, *We* are

Saint Germain and El Morya

Through Lah Rahn Ananda 08-30-2011

Tuning up Your Vibrations
~ Applied Spirituality from Saint Germain ~

EGO Behavior *compared with*	**Your Highest-Self Choices**

EGO Behavior

"My small story is what counts!" Over dramatizes.
  Is selfishly focused, ignoring Unity consciousness.
  Ego confuses its small story with Reality!
Indulges in *fear-based behavior.* including fear.

Strives to be "important". The BIG shot! Greedy!

"I'm always right" attitude. Arrogant. Believes
Ego's *opinion* is correct! Ignores Human fallibility.
Re-enforces the sagging self-esteem by denial.

My opinion, i.e., "*my* truth", is *the* Truth!!!
"There are no other possibilities but mine!"
Self-Aggrandizes. *Dominates* selfishly
to over- ride or restrict others' Free-will choices.

Makes untenable excuses. Projects the blame
onto another one/thing. "It's someone else's fault".
Avoids accountability and responsibility.

Complains about **unfulfilled expectations**.
Demands *immediate* satisfaction!
Prefers *complaining* to implementing solutions!
  Gets "stuck" on irreconcilable issues.
    Obsesses about dissatisfactions.

Escalates frustration into anger and hate.
Enjoys being angry; regards as acceptable!
Lets *impatience* accelerate into anger.
Believes anger or hate get the best results,
Uses anger to "bully" others, often hiding *fear.*
Promotes conflict and greed. Seeks revenge.

Unable and or unwilling to *recognize emotions
  in action.*

A prisoner of its own device.

Your Highest-Self Choices

Overcomes EGO's burning indulgences, replacing
these with *aligned self-choices for highest good.*
Learns, applies, *and* remembers life's lessons,
*Embraces this process with empathy and love, with Light
  overshining fear of change.*
Knows Joy through *humility and helpfulness.*

**Seeks truth, applying the merit of different
Perspective(s)** to each moment of every day life.
Replaces denial with reality and self-integrity!

Discerns the *difference* between the EGO's
belief system and *Universal/Divine Law/Truth.*
Seeks Mastery of Spirit's teachings of love and truth.
See Alchemy and Freedom, Saint Germain's **booklet.**

Knows truth and accepts reality with Joy.
Pacifies an untamed EGO into submission
into its rightful role. Promotes harmony.

Demonstrates patience by shrinking the EGO's
stature, now relegated *to take a back seat.*
Seeks out and implements creative solutions, thus
replacing complaints without squandering energy.
Expresses gratefulness. Sees Blessings! 4th Ed.

Utilizes Saint Germain's   LightOmeter
healing techniques as presented in His book
       "Flight of the Soul".

Consciously *recognizes* behavior in real-time.
Elevates negative emotions, raising them up into Neutral or Positive Zones
Is accountable.   See 10th Ed.
Fully ENJOYS the Mastery and rewards *of aligned actions.*

Discovers the Human Condition!
Transcends the Human Illusion!!

Honors the Birthright of One's own evolved Human Spirit!

**Aligns consciousness with Universal/Divine Law,
freeing your Highest-Self to BE.**

"To Truly Be or not to BE is Your Question". Saint Germain
Through Lah Rahn Ananda 05/2010

Growing To Fill Your Divine Business Shoes

*From Saint Germain
and Lah Rahn Ananda*

Greetings once again, Chelas, Light Workers, and Students of Spirit. Some in your World would define success as simply the attainment of wealth. A Divining Soul who knows the vastly expanded definition of success, however, will fully embrace the Masterful evolution of the Soul. By placing within your devoted consciousness the gifts of Masterful behavior set forth in this Edition, your career journeys can be lightened and infused with joy in exchange for shouldering needless self-inflicted burdens.

I come this day, along with My signatory Earth-Partner and Representative, to assist you now in steering your ship upon its optimum course at this juncture … to embrace your ever mounting Soul opportunities, simultaneously with the surrender of an ordinary Earth-life into *extraordinary* Divine moments, business journeys and careers which We now address.

In this transmission, We support you to use the *best possible focus and clarity* in the coming weeks, months and years, (and beyond, of course). *Wise use of your time* now combined with prudent actions will bear heavily upon either upward movement *or* status quo dormancy in the upcoming cycles of your Earthly business pursuits.

Herein, We advise and coach you to diligently employ certain underlying "core values" which in turn can over-shine your thoughts, motives, plans, intentions, actions, and overall behavior as you venture forth.

We acknowledge that Change can be a confrontive challenge, yet transmuted into a heartfelt rewarding phenomenon, if emotions are consistently moved into the "positive zone of emotional responses" and held there. (My Ascension Training Book, Flight of the Soul, Saint Germain, 2010.) **Believe Us when We say** *"change shall become part of your name(s) in the near and distant future"*.

Especially important now for your future and for that of your Planet is the quality of the people with whom you do business. This needs your focused and immediate attention. Bear in mind that relationships that continue to be supported by the Ascended Masters must incorporate, at a minimum, *integrity, wisdom,* professionalism, professional ethics, honesty, and appropriate connection to the Divine business at hand. Yes, you are capable of this. It is the Law for higher advancement into the Realm.

We want you to know that your Soul has beckoned Ascended Spirit for many Earth years in this lifetime to approach Us and to become One with God, embraced in Spirit's arms. Until about a score of years ago, many of you knew not of how to find your way, except for mundane daily chores and activities of an *ordinary unexamined* Earth life.

You must now be informed that many Souls have asked the Ascended Realm, and Myself as Saint Germain, in particular, to be their Ascended Spirit guide in this lifetime. I have chosen One of My Earth-Partners, now incarnated for a time, as the instrument with whom you are now working, to be your incarnated Spirit Guide for this journey. Here, we shall polish you up a bit, perhaps to the point of emerging as a shining demonstration for your colleagues, customers, and fellow Chelas.

If you have been chosen by One of the other Ascended Masters in My realm, then I, as Maha Chohan, applaud your connection and most lovingly defer to that Enlightened Master of Spirit to embrace you. In any event, as you listen on, your Soul presently *seeks to have your current Human belief system rise up in this lifetime* to fully realize *your Soul's ascended level of true and affectionate Trust and Faith in the Holy Spirit.*

Fortunately, in your present Earth-life, some willing Soul has volunteered to introduce you to one of *Our Earthly instruments,* who graciously accepted the invitation to show up embodied, to meet you and bring Our energies into your auric field. This transmission is a result of such gracious service now brought to you.

In your growth process, some of you have chosen to show a remarkable appetite for exposure to the Holy Spirit and the Realms over which We preside. For some, your appetites for Spiritual growth have *transmuted into a sharp hunger* and thus We have been able to accelerate your process and work with you and to mold and serve your Highest-Self. *The ultimate purpose of this redirection is to facilitate your serving the greater good of Humanity in concert with your Spiritual evolvement.* If this is your history, you and your Soul are to be commended for this flexibility in overcoming common Human resistance, taking significant steps toward Spirit. If your history is one of persistent resistance to Spirit and stagnated patterns, We pray your lamentable Ego attachments will soon give way to some measure of progress.

If My *former commendation marks your history,* you *may* have qualified to be most grandly embraced by Spirit, as a result of your *Free-will submission to Spirit's guidance* and your agreement to serve in confluence with Divine Law. We pray for your continued enrollment and admirable *Free-will submission* to the Will of Spirit. (See other Chronicle Editions clarifying aligned use of Free-will, while preserving your right of choice).

Abiding with Spirit will greatly affect the Grace of your future in this lifetime and specifically accelerate your growth to now fulfill your Divine business shoes, if that be your choice.

GROUNDING YOUR FUTURE BEYOND THE PAST

A few words now to set the stage for moving forward.

As We launch into this often tangled web, it would be well to examine the life-tracks you have left imprinted in the sands of your past, wearing your "old Business shoes" … and then to mark, in all Self-honesty, the milestone you now stand upon. And then, of course, to chart a new course, modified or reinforced by these findings that are uncovered.

Can you uncover your life's-tracks?

We know that all Humans are immensely *tested* by the temptations of greed and fear embedded in the Human survival condition. This is to be expected. Your past *could be well marked* by the effects of these tests, as you have interrelated and acted in the Business sector of your Earth-World relationships.

What the Ascended Realm asks of you now is to identify your past patterns where you have deviated from the aligned Divine and Universal Laws in order to forward your own agendas, largely ignoring a higher purpose in favor of your own small agenda!

Be brutally honest with yourself in this process, as that will open the door for constructive change. *Self-deception* will spill the wind out of your sails here and sink ye old ship into the briny deep, mates. Recall major incidents and actions where you would, in retrospect, have acted differently. Write these down to review. Then review!

What is past is done (although a *clean-up* may well be in order in some cases). We focus here upon the present opportunities to alter course and to now chart a new course for your future actions, thoughts, decisions, and behaviors … and your Karma.

Indeed, Spirit and your Highest-Self may feel some past actions to be reprehensible, culpable upon many planes, and out of Divine alignment. Your golden treasure in this hunt is to recognize, identify, release guilt, and take the pledge with Us to be fully engaged in this present process, telling all the while the full truth to yourself. We already know!

> **Know this. *We are not here this day to judge your past but to heal your future before it is acted out!***

Self-forgiveness for certain past deeds (not your defensive justifications) is the starting point of healing in these matters. And then …… comes the *Promise Pledged!*

That would be NOW!

Remember, in the end you are accountable unto Spirit and to your own Soul which beckons your evolvement and surrender to integrity and truth … in this lifetime of choices.

> **Most assuredly, We Ascended judge not your trek and quest for the gold, but rather the Way you go about it.**
>
> **So, retract any claws that may protrude as you climb toward the top of the pile … in favour of a graceful ascent wrapped with OUR Blessings and Grace all along your path. Rewards shall find you.**

OUTSIDE OF YOUR COMFORT ZONE

By this point, if you are authentically engaged with Us here, you will no doubt feel a squirrely restlessness taking hold. Be advised that this state of vulnerability is the location of your golden treasure … the growth in consciousness you seek. Once attained, you will be led into Divine Manifestation. It's a sad truth mates, the pecking order here is the egg, then the chicken, then the golden egg!

> In short, We ask that you travel here with Us to a destination of honesty and Self-commitment within yourself where YOU are restfully alert and willing to be
>
> far *outside of your comfort zone!*

THIS EVOLVED SPACE IS THE ZONE OF GROWTH AND POTENTIAL REWARDS.

Sound ironical? Perhaps in the beginning … until you learn to step outside of the box and connect your own dots!

We are leading up to Change and Re-Alignment here, my good and fine feathered friends. Any and all business tactics and behavior that are out of Divine Alignment will need to be CHANGED and this requires your immediate attention. Change, *someday more convenient,* will not suffice to receive Our Blessings of Grace and Endorsement.

And yes, … such immediate Change is boldly confrontive to a belief system that has little regard for the integrity of its *means as* long as its END is accomplished.

Sound familiar? This dark modus operandi must be unbolted and CHANGED once and for good. The end does not necessarily justify the means, Folks!

In addition, on a grander scale, *collective consciousness* Change begins with individuals like you, Dear Ones.

Have any of you wondered why your Blessings may be so sparse these days?

Join hands with Us now, allow your Free-will to be in Divine Partnership, and step lightly wearing your new Business shoes that hold a higher vibration to serve an astounding new purpose for you while you are watched over from above.

WHY WOULD YOU WEAR THESE SHOES?

Is it possible that these shoes could cushion your feet to guide you to walk your Dharma, where Business becomes a vehicle for a Soul's learning of indispensable Soul lessons through the mere mechanism of Earth-money?

Ponder this a moment!! Then re-read.

Yes, you have been *duped with money* in the grander sense. Your quest and fascination for gold does indeed have, beyond the obvious and essential Earthly purpose it serves, a deeper Divine use and higher purpose vastly beyond the desperate quest, the seizing, and the clutching of the gold itself. Would philanthropy be an option?

Are you "outside of the box" yet? Let us continue.

GROWTH AND CHANGE

Now, comes the test of Change and more Change. We suggest you make yourself a *Friend of Change*. This has been stated many times. You can gracefully receive Our assistance here.

> **Collapsing into an *Ego's uncontrolled urges for acting alone* without asking for Spirit's Wisdom and consultation input is a juicy temptation for Ones who may have freshly tasted the sweetness of a 1st success!**

Acting alone while wedded in Divine Partnership is a dangerous road to travel as Blessings and Grace are thus deliberately *put at risk*, once you know better. Behavior of acting alone will sometimes reappear *after* having had a sample of *Our abilities to dispense Blessings and Grace through Divine Power.*

Such acting alone is a deviation from Divine Law and often produces a temporary illusion of a Human's *imagined new powers* and heightened Self-esteem, saying "I have the power now and I'm fully in charge", "I no longer need Spirit's Blessings".

Behaviors can then escalate further into inauthenticity, reckless decision-making, inappropriate emoting, acting out, bragging, boasting, Self-aggrandizing, ignoring humility, ungratefulness, disregarding Laws of the Divine and of Man, etc. etc.

AVOIDING THESE TRAPS *of regression and collapse is the transmutational order of the day for you. Just so you do not feel unduly singled out,* <u>please know that all of Our Chela students face these same issues and countless more. Their issues are just encased in different packages, bound by unique strings in different belief systems.</u> We work lovingly with all Ones in Human incarnation, Ones <u>*authentically*</u> *enrolled in the Earth-School of Spirit,* reshaping and molding their belief systems to coincide with Universal and Divine Law.

These Ones choose to be chosen.

Engaging yourself in *full use of the keys* We provide will open doors of *suitable opportunities* beyond your visible horizons. We urge you always to seek and implement solutions which embrace a win-win philosophy and outcome f*or all 3 business participants in the Divine Partnership.* You need to hold this Sacred relationship foremost in your mind and heart! *Follow Our lead, and you will be astonished* (you already could be to some extent) at the fine results, love, and worthy new Self-esteem that can come unto you in the form of Blessings and Grace. Some who read here already know of what We speak! Some have strong faith but need proof.

When Grace blesses your life, you will know!

Comte Saint Germain
Portrait by Nicolas Thomas, 1783 public domain

> We in Spirit demonstrate the finest manner of living an exemplary Human life-style, regardless of your *aligned and chosen* Earthly profession. You are invited to come in and join Us daily.

ABOUT CHANGE

Yes, change is surrounding you upon all sides as you are experiencing and deeply feeling in a chaotic Earth-World. Your meditation practice is highly recommended at this time and must continue. You are urged to set and reserve a regular clock-time each morning, and meditate before any work is commenced. This will help to focus and ground you, for at least a breather, in the beginning of the day. Regular routines are healthy and recommended for Earth workers and inhabitants, young and old.

<u>Your</u> *daily discipline will be required* here for Us to coach you along further on your Dharmic path, where *some Ones* of you shall begin to commune with Ourselves in greater depth. *Others* will choose to stay stuck in their Ego's illusion that says <u>the payoff</u> for maintaining the status quo of their morass-filled consciousness <u>exceeds</u> Our loving offer of Blessings and Grace and Spiritual evolution in this lifetime.

HUMAN INTERACTIONS

As We have put forth to you on repeated occasions, continued progress in your new career endeavors depends in a great part upon your learning to polish up your *skills of Human interactions,* advancing these soon into *effective* capabilities of synchronizing events between individuals, participants, groups, and institutions, … such that interactions with yourself begin to intermesh in harmony, *without great effort on your part.* Your interpersonal relationships are meant to be pleasant, effective, emotionally balanced, and to serve your highest aligned purpose with honor. *You can be Master of your emotions or let your emotions be Master of you! Which are you?*

As you interact with colleagues, clients and contacts, *the professional manner and heightened <u>vibrations housed in your voice and body</u>* are of gargantuan importance to your success. Now is your chance to learn, and then to shine, Dear Ones! You are born to shine!

The unalterable standards of supreme ethics of which We speak must also be forever practiced and delivered without exception. Such ingrained and automatic behavior (inward thoughts and outward behaviors) shall hold you in the finest regard with colleagues and Our recognition for preservation of your <u>*Sacred Divine Partnership with the Holy Spirit.*</u>

BALANCE, STABILITY AND PROGRESS

Progressing in this arena requires a delicate balance so you can devotedly see the various scenarios of Earth business from *all perspectives, not just from your own;* namely, from that of your customer(s), your society, and from the eyes of the established institutions, and then from the Divine perspective that governs in the end.

> We are saying that you must stand in several pairs of shoes at the same time, being aware of the needs and wishes of each. When you widen your scope of vision, you will be more able to see the end from the beginning, where minds of Free-will will have the opportunity to meet, as in manifesting signed, goodfaith contracts! Remember your objectives!

You must learn about timing and priority of events as they present themselves, and to constantly adapt as events change in character and profile. Remember things do not always *continue to appear* as they may have appeared at the first glance through any number of apparitions in your consciousness.

Also, as We have attempted to teach you, … the skill of staying *always* <u>on top of your game</u> is a requirement for any professional, <u>versus just reacting from moment</u> to moment to what has just occurred and hoping to make the best of it …… ASSUMING that somehow you can extricate yourself from the wreckage and salvage the ruins that need not have happened in the inception!

We speak here of anticipating needs, questions, structures and solutions etc. before they may be put to you, right "in your face" as you would say. <u>It is called dynamic</u>

anticipation. Your Alexander the Great was and is famously known for masterfully applying these skills … to *plan, act, anticipate, react and adapt* in most admirable and timely ways. Do you know that Aristotle was his teacher? Your Human history can teach you greatly if you will allow it. Do you know that two of *My prior Human lifetime incarnations were those of William Shakespeare and Socrates?*

A marketing professional and business dealmaker sometimes has only the *brief moments in the situation* to create a suitable solution while on the stage! *Anticipation and being fully prepared* can convert a frightened panic-in-crisis moment into a marvelous opportunity to allay fears and then to present a grand solution that fits perfectly like a fine leather glove. We speak here to endorse solutions that are fully aligned with the Divine intention.

Integrating these skills will come in time with insight, dedication and perseverance. And yes, perfect practice does make perfect. Within this integration, keenly distinguish among objective, process, and intended outcome. Wisdom embraces Dreams!

Only trained professionals are up to the task of delivering at this level. We pray, in due course, to include you among this group as you progress into such Mastery.

So, in your business dealings, We suggest that you begin immediately to wisely apply all of the above Wisdom. This can not be deferred until SOME DAY later. Your Earth-time is of the essence. Some day has arrived … it is now. Harness the power of your present moments, Dear Ones.

MANAGING GROUPS

Now, regarding the management of Groups in a business arrangement, and the individuals within each such group, this will require *some additional skills on your part.* These you must learn well.

Because of the Human Condition being such as it is, with DNA and all of its fear and greed bubbling at the surface, it is paramount that you control and carefully tailor your words to each of the individuals *within each Business Group* … all the while maintaining your full level of integrity.

And further, that you show Self-control about information you *pass between one Business Group and another such group.* Group individuals may well not be meant to even know each other or of the roles that each may play.

This discipline requires skillful application of the "Need to Know" rule. Use it diligently! Starting now. Think before you speak! *Learn to hear Spirit in the moment before you speak.* Revealing too much unnecessary information to the wrong individual(s) can rapidly destroy any good progress you have made toward the intended objective!

Let me be clear. Conformance with Divine Law absolutely does require *full disclosure of all relevant* facts, speaking the Truth, and contracting in Good Faith. Here, We alert you of the danger in *loose business conversations*, chats, and indulgence in revealing extraneous information that is not required to comply with Divine requirements and *to successfully complete a transaction at hand.*

So, in your people-interactions, fine feathered Friends, beware that your Ego may want to "show off" and tell people how much you know and how brilliant "you" have become, especially when a new success is freshly in place.

Your Ego will want to say "I told you so, that I could do it" … despite others' discouraging words and doubts. The Ego will delight in "rubbing your success in people's faces", an emotion wanting to say "I am better than you … so take that!", etc. etc. *This is just a sagging, and often desperate, low Self-esteem trying to rise up and gain a shred of an imagined new Self-dignity.*

Dignity and respect are earned and deserved through your suitable behavior, good Ones … not earned through business success alone.

The Ascended Realm observes Egos of unbelievable sizes and shapes, wildly aggrandizing and justifying themselves, all to feed their insecurities rooted in fear and greed.

Do I have your attention? Are you following Me? Re-read?

Re-reading this transmission in full will be necessary at least six (6) times over and then monthly thereafter as a scheduled event in your calendar. *Such reviews will compound the benefits you shall receive and enjoy as you wear your new Divine business shoes.*

COURSE CHANGES AND ADJUSTMENTS

The antidote and Divine Prescription here is to replace all of this Ego-indulgent nonsense with a hearty dose of Humility and Gratefulness! As Saint Germain, I assure you *that Divine Blessings are directly connected* to your success in correcting untamed Ego urges and transferring this energy into a focus upon the guidance of Spirit.

Alright. <u>*Let us continue and speak now about your reputation.*</u> We intend you are held in a favorable view.

In keeping with this intention, you must become forcefully aware that business people *you associate with* all *have their own set of morals*, both light and dark in your Earthly duality. You must understand this and <u>distance yourself accordingly</u>.

When you affiliate with individuals or companies and in turn *introduce them to one another*, your reputation is at stake!! (in addition to the Group dynamics We just spoke about). Therefore, you must weed out and <u>disassociate yourself from the questionable ones</u>! This discipline could test your abilities to detach from any and all individuals/groups who somehow strangely attract you and yet, at times, are sourced by dark energies.

Beware of your Self-defeating feelings overtaking your best instincts of Highest-Self! It's called Self-sabotage.

If you can *learn to accurately access Wisdom* from your Highest-Self, you can easily avoid Self-defeating associations at the start! *This access will require training.*

<u>An unstable Ego</u> can easily and "comfortably" <u>revert to seeking out lower levels of business or social contacts when carelessness or desperation sets in</u>. Chelas can learn to exclude rather than mistakenly include associations who have previously shown themselves to lack the integrity, capability or character. *Know that contacts of the highest character are the very ones deserving of you and those which the Ascended Masters require.*

Key relationships may abandon you if your appearance in <u>reputation</u> by association becomes tarnished (justly or unjustly) by way of having referred or recommended or introduced an *unworthy individual to a most worthy and valued ally*, for example. Stinky stigmas can rub off on you and be very difficult to remove, once that happens. People remember!

So, beware not to stain your own Honor! As your Chinese friends would say "act to honor yourself." In short, you shall become known partially by the Quality of those with whom you do <u>business</u> and also those you allow in <u>your social circle(s)</u> as well. We will address refinement of social circles in a later transmission.

> **Consulting Spirit at every turn and asking guidance is the wise course of a rising Chela. "Going it alone" can have grave consequences, once you know better.   Nota Bene.**
>
> **Attaining the skill to lend your ear and <u>hear</u> the Voice of Spirit, and to hear Us <u>accurately</u>, My dear Friends, is entirely another subject, addressed elsewhere in this *Saint Germain Chronicle Collection*, which you now**
>
> **hold in your hands.**

Some of you are trusting Souls and are sometimes easily duped. We hope to assist you in *wise* choices made in dynamic real-time. Greater discernment will serve you.

<u>You must learn to believe that which is worthy of belief!</u>

So have a care about not only the words you speak out BUT also about the people with whom you associate or introduce to each other, and the possible consequences of their respective interactions.

We speak specifically of ethics, honesty, motives and scruples of your business contacts and associates, <u>*especially in your inner circle.*</u>

<u>*Costly mistakes* of association in business and social circles</u> can be avoided *using skills of insight* that We ask you to develop, and insights you know by now that can be gleaned from consulting Spirit, sometimes with a simple phone call.

<u>TAKING OUR MESSAGE TO HEART</u>

I suggest you FULLY take this message to heart. Compliance will speed your journey into happy and satisfying manifestations and realizations of your aligned dreams. Careless or reckless behavior can, on the contrary, cause grief and damage sometimes beyond repair, <u>even from the Ethers</u>.

Intaking all that is written here admittedly will be a BIG GULP for you. You are not meant to choke, but rather to let this energy lay in to your consciousness piece by piece.

<u>*This requisite diligence is* "on you" *as Humans would say.*</u> Coaching a Human consciousness into the higher Dimension(s) takes years and yet some can move along quickly, <u>if without Ego fanfare</u>. Your choice. Once transmitted, *this information and energy* is your responsibility to be applied to your Being. It may not be repeated. So

Seize the Day, good Ones! Use this Chronicle as a handy reference, close at hand, if you are wise.

Tap yourself upon the shoulder, as a reminder, that this entire Chronicle transmission is targeted for all Spiritual Devotees, <u>whatever your perceived level of evolvement</u>, as a cleansing and recurring WAKEUP CALL.

Very importantly, We ask that you NOT MEMORIZE Our words here but simply inflow the energy into your consciousness so that you cement the wisdom and conform your way of Being in daily practice to the standards enveloped in the Divine Will. Your Soul knows about the Divine Will! Begin having Soul consultations with your Earth-Self and you will be amazed about the outcomes.

Once new patterns are cemented in place, We can build further upon this foundation to accelerate your journey into higher dimensions of *positive Karma which your Soul beckons you to attain in this lifetime upon Earth. Spirit yearns to speed your journey onward.*

> **So We say again, "bear in mind that relationships which continue to be supported by the Ascended Masters must incorporate, at a minimum, integrity, wisdom, professionalism, ethics, honesty, and appropriate connection to the Divine business at hand."**

As for the *Magic of Manifestation,* I say to you as Saint Germain, that this complex feat is a subject beyond the scope and gift of this Chronicle Edition, though inextricably entwined with *Growing to Fill Your Divine Business Shoes.* This particular Chronicle Edition lays a <u>vital part of your foundation</u> for *subsequent instruction surrounding Manifestation. After you have Mastered Our gifts offered here,* seek out and find my past works embracing this marvelous phenomenon of Manifestation with all of its mystery, harmony, and *Alchemical magic.*

My many transmissions on *Alchemy and Manifestation* will guide you further in this vein, once you have mined the gold herein. I send you good cheer in *ultimately realizing your Mastery of Manifestation,* a Human accomplishment of Divine delight.

An Earth journey is a long trek by Human measures, and therefore, We urge you to take the best of care of your physical health and mental well-being as you rise up to the apex of Mastering Our highest standards.

And We say "Manifest your Divine Dreams."

We in Spirit have every confidence that you will succeed in grand fashion. Call upon the Ascended Realm at any moment in time or space.

In Divine service of Humanity, I AM

Saint Germain
with Lah Rahn Ananda

MARKETING MANIFESTATION

~ 3rd DIMENSIONAL PLANE ASPECTS ~

Marketing Professionals face common challenges in acquiring Prospects, then converting them into Qualified Clients, and finally closing the sale with a bona fide contract.

This 3-D portion of the sequence addresses only part of the process, as the endorsement and Magical Blessing of the Ascended Realm of Spirit is also in this equation, granted or not to a Spiritual Devotee depending, in part, upon the situation's Divine alignment with Light in the eyes of Spirit. While oversimplified here, this is the sum and substance of the matter, for Ones involved in such Earthly ventures in your Duality. Be aware that Spirit surely notes the underlying, ultimate purpose and intention of your endeavor! You are well advised to pay heed … as *you* then seek to be paid … to the following major Marketing Phases commonly encountered in this sequential process:

Contact

Contribution

Commitment

Conversion

Closing

Contract

Commission

As you wrap your thoughts and actions around these elements of the marketing process, gift yourself by filling in your own blanks behind each distinct phase. This is up to you. Note that if a phase is omitted, ignored, or unfulfilled, your project will likely need to be started anew or just simply end. *Lessons of experience shall prevail*, good Friends and Chelas. **Good fortune in the Light.**

Saint Germain and Lah Rahn Ananda 07-2014

Affirmation of Abundance

I AM loving creation and abundance
walking joyfully
through the open door of suitable opportunity

I AM loving creation and abundance
walking joyfully
through the open door of suitable opportunity.

May your path be sprinkled with Angel dust
as you make this affirmation
Yours in a daily practice.

Saint Germain

The Saint Germain Chronicles
Tenth Edition Transmitted on 02-27-2013

HEALTH MATTERS

 N this day, I shall underscore a topic which competes on Humanity's challenging list for a top position of merit-worthy free-will choices. I AM speaking of physical, mental, and Spiritual well-being health practices, and the *life's priorities* you wisely *set into your Self-supportive daily schedule.*

Greetings from Above.

This Edition of the *Saint Germain Chronicles* is vitally important to you All in this *Earth-time of massive change and of Human stress behaviors.*

Your invitation:

To read HEALTH MATTERS several times over, as if it were your *first exposure*. And then, post it upon the door of your refrigerator, from which you withdraw wisely chosen nutrients.

Our energies here are directed *to penetrate consciousness and open pathways for intaking that which could otherwise meet resistance.*

Human well-being includes a state of *Perfect Healing,* **which We intend to share with All ... and yet, Chelas can, nonetheless, respond to Our offers with Self-defeating walls of behavior, blocking the potential strengths and healings** *that beckon to enfold you in luminous, radiant clouds of White Light that await. These Blessings can be yours, as you act to align.*

Would you be agreeable to accept Our loving guest invitation to now cast *daily attention* toward your personal life-pivotal HEALTH MATTERS and longevity? We shall hold the whispers of Our etherical breath, awaiting your *response in action*.

We have been known to guide Chelas *in such choices,* which will forward you in being ready for your next Earthly assignments. Your alignment with Our suggestions and directives is the forerunner of synchronicities and Blessings that inevitably follow. In the beginning and sometimes later, the arrival and realization of this truth is difficult to comprehend, yet those of continued Faith gain the rich experiences of Grace in the end. When, says the impatient Ego? That is up to you.

Yes, *distractions from merit worthy choices, surrounding Health Matters in this case,* will inevitably be cobblestones along the path of your growth and evolution into higher consciousness. Be heartfully aware of these choices as they occur, even though sometimes as distractions. Your finely attuned ability to *re-adjust* your choices of behavior in the present moment *will be key to the essential progress I pray will be yours in perfect health.*

At the present moment of this reading, *your most pressing choice* is your decision to focus and concentrate attention upon your health.

This will be an on-going assignment for you during the remainder of this Earth-life incarnation. Surely, and in self-love, *set this priority in place* from this day forward. *Accept at this time, if you will, Our higher vibrations of Spiritual nourishment surrounding your overall health, over-shined by Our unconditional love for you. Are you aware that your matters of health include not only the selection of food and drink (and your drugs that you may ingest),* *but also your mental health? … along with the thoughts that you choose to engage with, and the choices you make in dealing with inevitable emotions that are constantly streaming in? These are all vital parts of your* <u>Health Package that Matters</u>*!* **Cleansing the mind often surfaces as a more daunting task than merely purging the body with a cathartic physic.**

This advice is not to be regarded as some whimsical or trite action that We temporarily recommend, nor to be once done and simply dismissed because it suits your fancy. <u>Health practices and discipline are not always convenient</u>! And yet, constructive choices will pay massive (awesome, as you say) dividends if performed on a regular daily basis! Can you not see how this regimen runs parallel to daily practice of meditation?

A regular routine of health practices needs be an every day event, Dear Friends! Can you also see that this is a matter of Self-love? The test here is to <u>transcend your Ego's comfort zone of convenience</u> and bravely stand up to the task of Self-preservation and Self-improvement. We can assist, but the initiative is squarely resting upon your shoulders.

This very moment of Truth confronts your continued well-being … the moment here, embraces your challenging task of learning to *live comfortably in your own skin … physically, mentally and emotionally!* We have spoken of this to you in years past. Do you remember?

Coupled with the forgoing is the unavoidable, sometimes inconvenient and inherent, responsibility of **Self-health,** *most Spiritually* incumbent upon all incarnated Humans. Many of you choose to ignore your health maintenance <u>until a breakdown occurs</u>.

Then, all too often, repair becomes an unnecessarily overwhelming task, or even a condition irreparable! However, We shower miraculous Blessings of Grace where Divine Law permits, to lighten your load.

To expand a bit, I say the choice of joy, or burden* of a Chela's health responsibility ultimately resides with that very Chela!** The Health System is available to serve you, and yet the **task** is yours to willingly reach out and accept the gifts that are presented. ***Your Self-Health is Our wish for you and yet not the responsibility of this Realm. I hasten to add, once again, that We will extend Our loving and merciful hands to you whenever GOD's Law dictates. This offer of manifested compassion, however, *relieves you of no responsibility whatsoever!* Do We have your keen attention by now?

Appreciate that Your mind, body and Soul blend as One into the Sacred Temple in which you dwell. This magnificent and beautiful arrangement of energies is a Spiritual phenomenon to be fully embraced and honoured by you. With repetitious diligence and re-reading of this Chronicle Edition, your consciousness and Ego shall have more than an even chance to Master surrender and thence be uplifted. It is up to you.

We shall elaborate upon specific areas of health focus for you in a personal reading to follow this **wake-up** transmission, if you choose to request a private audience with Ourselves.

Know this:

<u>**Health issues, left neglectfully untreated and unhealed,**</u> <u>enter the Karmic realm for that Chela.</u> We speak of matters such as: unhealed wounds, active infection, lingering infection, obesity, lack of exercise, obsessive behaviors, indulgent diets, sleep deprivation, undisciplined mental processes, emotional breakdowns, lack of meditation, indulgent daily habits, lack of nourishment and timely hydration, etc. You have a pressing need to be most attentive to current health care directives from your qualified health professionals, to be responsible for health insurance for your care, for preventive measures, and for a myriad of other specifics, too extensive for this moment. **Health Matters**, once Mastered, will reward you with comfort, satisfaction, joy and peace of mind, believe Me. *Here, in this space of Grace, you will discover that living an exemplary Human lifestyle does bear most delicious fruits!*

For extended rewards of life's pleasures and joys, We say to you: ACTION, FOCUS AND ATTENTION is needed. We Ascended trust that your *correct choices* will be initiated soon, and then followed by *decisive and wise actions* as an integral part of your daily regimen (systematic course of treatment). My Dear Ones, … *unattended* and ignored health issues can become chronic, affecting the quality of *your entire remaining Earth-life.* Managing your health care is part of <u>**being your own Best Friend, and a Friend of Change**</u>.

I say, "Seek out the Joys of Change and Behold thy Friend."

Alright, enough in this moment. Heed well, My Dear Friends, and continue in true Partnership with Ourselves, as is Our full intention and healing prayer for You.

In Unconditional Love and Light, I AM

Saint Germain
for All the Realm

Through Lah Rahn Ananda

*In the Dance of Life it is Grace
that Dances on Bandaged Feet.*
Author unknown

Amazing Grace

Amazing grace, how sweet the sound
    That saved a wretch like me!
    I once was lost
    But now I Am found
    Was blind but now I see
    T'was grace that taught my heart to fear
    And grace my fears relieved
    How precious did that Grace appear
    The hour I first believed!

Through many dangerous toils and snares
    I have already come
    'Tis Grace has brought me safe thus far
    And Grace will lead me home
    When we've been there ten thousand years
    Bright shining as the sun
    We've no less days to sing God's praise
    Than when we'd first begun.

Text by John Newton and John Ross
Music by Virginia Harmony, 1831,
Public Domain

Eleventh Edition   Transmitted on 02-27-2013

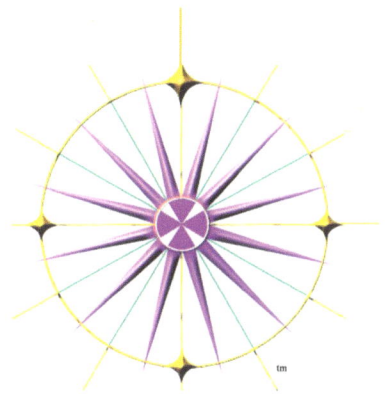

The Manifesting Power of Each Moment

This Saint Germain Decree has 7 verses or stanzas which need to be recited in sequential order. Below the verses, you will find Saint Germain's illumination and explanation of the essence of each verse to assist you. Be well and inhale higher vibrations with each breath as you Decree.

Blessings.

Decree

I AM the Manifesting Power of Each Moment.

I AM joyfully willing to love, care for, and accept
each new moment of my life as it unfolds.

I AM courage, I AM clarity, I AM abundance.

I AM the surrendered practice of visible
Manifestation, humbly unfolding
in this ordinary secular world.

I AM Light and Love gratefully radiating itself.

I AM the heartbeat of the Universe as I now
Manifest, Manifest, Manifest.

I AM One with the One.

I AM the Manifesting Power of Each Moment.

"Here rests a quintessential element of your Divine Self.

This <u>Alchemical Power</u>, once earned and internalized … through study, repetition, selfless dedication to Spirit, much disciplined and obedient listening to our guidance from above … becomes the bloom of your *extraordinary* growth.

Like the rose, you can open up your true beauty for all the sentient world to see. Your purposes need be selfless and directed toward the benefit of Humanity; there may or may not be personal benefit in your intended purpose(s), when viewed through the eyes of *your own perspective.*

Please shower yourself with kindness and read My book on Alchemy once you have Mastered this Gift of Decree that you now read. Wisely use the Power of Manifestation in *full* alignment, and Grace will surround your actions always."

I AM joyfully willing to love, care for, and accept *each* new moment of my life as it unfolds.

"In this state, and in this presence, you are aligned with the vibration of creation, … you are opened to receive from the higher dimensions. Here you are joyfully responsible for the unfolding of your own Divine adventure in concert with your Choices.

Honor this highly coveted Earthly legacy with all the strength you can muster from your Earth consciousness and your Highest-Self, illuminated by the fire of your internal sun, the Holy Spirit. This is your *Divine Partnership.*"

I AM courage
I AM clarity
I AM abundance.

"This affirmation bears the powerful specificity that manifestation requires, and which Alchemy rewards. Hold dear the energy of these words in your daily walks and meditations."

I AM the surrendered practice of visible manifestation, humbly unfolding in this ordinary secular world.

"*In this state of higher consciousness*, the passion of your aligned thoughts turned to action possess you unmistakably, … to carry out 110 % of your part of the Divine Partnership. This level of commitment combined with a most *heartful surrender* to the ultimate outcome will inevitably Grace your life. This is your Blessing. It is the Law! It is My Honor.

Alchemy in practice on Earth often demands your positive engagement action with agreeable forces and energies of the Dimension in which you reside. Coupled thusly with aligned intentions, Our Masterful synchronicities may then be offered in Alchemical Grace.

Here is the test of patience, along with your Spiritual courage, come to the fore. The rewards of knowing a sustained and unending connection with the Father, and Ourselves in the Masterful Realm as well, shall raise you above the peer pressures *urging you on to live an unexamined life that leads to nowhere but the repetitious Karmic cycle.*

Nothing is more noble **to** *Me than a walking demonstration of all that I teach. Will You walk with Me in this surrendered practice of manifestation?"*

I AM Light and Love gratefully radiating itself.

"*When you truly walk with the Holy Spirit, you walk with the real You*, the grand Being you were sent here to Be in the flesh. Achieving this state of vibration requires the utmost Alchemical concentration, 24 x 7 (as you say) … for the rest of your Earth life this time around. I know there are those of you up to the task!"

I AM the heartbeat of the Universe as I now Manifest, Manifest, Manifest.

"Love is the Spark that ignites the flame in the Altar of Your Heart."

I AM One with the One.

"As you are forever engaged in the Sacred practice of this Oneness, ... So shall ye be with your Sacred Earth life, walking in step, synchronized with Me.

I invite you to

<u>Walk With Me</u> in this

Glorious Victory March as you

Manifest Your

FREEDOM!"

Saint Germain

Channeled Through Lah Rahn Ananda 2001, 2009

* **For your learning, use, and Mastery of this instructional Gift, Saint Germain suggests that you learn by heart *each* verse of this decree, adding one of the seven verses each consecutive week, so you end the process with the lasting ability to recite all the verses together, fully interconnected and fully connected to your *Self*. You have My kindest wishes for a Mysteriously Miraculous result.**

Lah Rahn Ananda (2001, 2009)

DEALING WITH YOUR FLUCTUATING EMOTIONS

reetings to All from the Ascended Realm.

Today, We superscribe with this excerpt, some salient points of great importance to you in dealing successfully with your Fluctuating Emotions, thus opening your *Beloved Gateway* into new, more peaceful, and harmonious states of consciousness by raising your vibration. Throughout the recorded history of your Earth-World, Mankind has struggled with learning to effectively manage its inborn emotions, *forever reappearing* as an integral God-given ingredient of the *Human condition*, embedded in your re-incarnation inheritance with each new Earth-life.

Soul Searching

In those dreamy and solitary moments of reflection, contemplate .... if you dare

What comes first, the Thought or the Feeling?

o

Who AM I under the mask I wear?

o

What is the focus of My Self-talk?

o

What is the Color of The Truth?

o

Rest assured, Dear Ones, your contemplations and musings are held in the vault of My Heart in the utmost confidence. Embrace your evolving reflections, as they occur over time, in your emerging and unique Grand Process.
Blessings in the Light,

El Morya *through Lek Rakn Ananda 2013*

Ascended Master El Morya and I, **as yours truly, come here now to show you through the Gateway**, the next step in Mastering your positive use of the emotions that flood your minds, bellies, and full bodies, … daily. These energies that *seemingly invade* your consciousness can truly be managed such that your full range of emotions are welcomed in by your belief system as they crop up in "real time", … as you say.

We observe that a number of embodied Earth Masters of Spirit at this Earth-moment have walked through Our Gateway and easily continue to maintain their vibrational status! To these walking Masters, incoming emotions offer no further threat or concern, *as their life's reactions are wisely and simply managed and balanced with effortless automaticity beyond the illusion that often grips you.* *This* Gateway path can lead you to such evolvement as well. If you are willing, as we proceed over your next 3 months, notice *your* progress in this regard as you *willingly choose to* put Our teachings into practice (momentarily, daily, and on-goingly). You will attract more Light and notice it! Others may notice it in you also, *without your prompting,* as you are a humble Being seeking evolvement and desiring not to self-aggrandize.

Once Mastered, your fluctuating range of emotions can *actually serve you well,* believe it or not! Ease and Grace follows Mastery, dear Friends. I AM speaking about the tangible quality of your daily Earth-life!

I speak of relationships, peace of mind, manifested results, harmony, self-confidence, and countless other parts of your life. Some core level training is required, however. Can you imagine how just a few of your challenging emotions could handily be transformed to serve you well? What would these be? Write some on paper now, perhaps before we proceed?

Now, about coupling clear recognition and identification of incoming/ongoing emotions with action. Our teachings combine this Self-observing discipline with conscious action to manage emotions. Application of this combination *will lead you into an unbelievable new space, peace, joy, and Blessings of Grace beyond your current beliefs*. This is a *promise* from above, if you follow My directions. And yes, there are conditions, as you might expect by now. Some of my well-known compulsory *corollaries are attached to My promise for your success*. So read on, good people. Many Monkeys will be lifted from your back, … burdens you have carried for years with no end in sight.

It should come as no surprise by now that climbing the rungs of the Spiritual ladder does, in fact, involve application of life-long energy of dedication, change and perseverance on the part of the aspiring Chela. Alright, let us continue.

Currently, the vast majorities of Human choices are made on a <u>*reactive basis*</u>, *ignoring* the <u>powerful potential of choosing to wisely manage emotions on a **conscious basis at the time the emotion presents**</u>!

Here now, We show you the way out of this dangerous reactive behavior trap, a pattern often entangling you in negative results showing up every Earth-day upon your *International stage* and upon your *own personal stage* where you are the actor, front and center.

You must accept the fact that entering this Gateway of Mastery and sustaining your position demands *the presence of a quiet mind*.

As noted in my *Flight of the Soul* book, daily Transcendental Meditation is one of your keys to opening the Gateway. Twenty to thirty Earth minutes <u>***per day in meditation***</u>, each and every day at a minimum, is a required step to maintaining the quiet mind. Ideally, for ambitious Chelas, two Transcendental Meditation sessions per day will accelerate your results. A positive habit, indeed!

Transcendental Meditation was put into practice centuries ago by Vedic priests and followers, who still practice Earthly world-wide "TM" en masse. This form of Meditation is simply a technique, folks. It releases the Human mind from its own prison of bombarding random thoughts into a fresh space of complete emptiness, opening that precious gateway of Purification and quiet harmony within. Your Buddhist practicners demonstrate this. As you begin your increasingly inviting daily Meditation(s), know that Vedic principles guide Humans to follow certain procedures:

Prepare for your meditation; eat your full meal afterward *or if you must*, eat a tiny bit prior, only a very light snack.

Early morning Meditations are encouraged as well as Meditation before your evening meal.

Start thinking Mantra, Mantra, Mantra now.

Sit comfortably in a straight back chair, spine straight, with arms and legs uncrossed, palms of hands open, and both feet fully planted flat on the floor or the Earth itself.

Welcome yourself into your Meditation session, looking forward to an enjoyable, relaxing treat.

Select a restful, peaceful, quiet environment with no distractions or sounds.

With eyes closed, begin silently saying to yourself in your mind your own personal Mantra. No movement of tongue or mouth.

Without effort, easily repeat your Mantra over and over. As you silently say your Mantra, you will notice random thoughts enter your mind and you then give attention to a thought. This is alright. Now, when **that one thought** is finished, return to repeating your Mantra. If you fall asleep, continue Meditation after sleep.

Repeat this process over and over and over, being aware to keep returning to your Mantra when a single thought is finished.

Note: this is a Meditation session, not a prayer session, or a time for you to tell Spirit and GOD about your ever-present, long list of things which you want Us to do for you!

Nor is this a free-for-all session where you choose to indulge in your rapid-fire emotional thoughts, pleasures, or worries, ignoring the saying of your Mantra.

Sakyamuni Buddha of Compassion

Chronicles@LightoftheSoul.org

This is Transcendental Meditation, where you choose your Mantra over your thoughts. This will take practice to Master, so be patient with yourself.

> **The accomplished Meditator will often remain in theta** brain wave state for several minutes at a stretch, <u>when this practice is perfected.</u>
>
> You will not be aware you are in the theta state while you are there. <u>Only after leaving this state will you realize that you</u> were there!

As this Mantra repetition progresses, you may notice there are fewer thoughts and more and more Mantra repetitions, now growing faint and ever more delicately refined, until there is no more of anything. *Simply emptiness, devoid of thoughts, pictures, or visions.* Nothing but pure presence, and without "concentration".

The theta state of Being simply IS. You must experience it to truly know. Here, the Meditator has taken a "dive" and can remain here for a time (seconds or minutes) until emerging, when the Mantra must be now repeated and used to restart this cycle again, and again, and again, each time leading to a duration of pure theta state consciousness. Sometimes, automatic breathing slows and seems to *almost* stop for several seconds at a stretch and then it resumes its slow rate again.

Physiological benefits of Transcendental Meditation are calculated, proven and beneficial for relationships and peace of mind. This technique is a healing process and <u>*not a psychological coping mechanism*</u>. Blood pressure, respiration rate, and body temperature, will often drop during Meditation, leaving One feeling rested and calm, often with the equivalent of 4 hours sleep.

Vedas recommend *slowly* opening the eyes and returning to full consciousness at the end of your allotted period. After two or three minutes, your daily routine is then resumed.

Professional Ayurvedic Meditation training is available from Vedic Centers in many major cities throughout the Earth-World.

<u>**To resume!**</u>

<u>**Thus equipped with a quiet mind, Mastery**</u> of these constantly recurring emotions will

become the pearls for your oyster garden, there for the harvest! Kindly remember that repetition of good habits yields character traits that are worthy of many Golden Blessings delivered at your feet. Each Beloved One that persists in applying Our teachings will become a living testamentary to that of which I speak. May I trust that you shall add your name?

In contrast, actions taken <u>where Emotional choices rule</u> over logic and more importantly over Divine guidance, these choices have clearly shaped the painful destinies of individuals *and* Nations throughout the history of Human inhabitance of your Earth. Do research, if you will. There are countless recorded cases of ill-advised emotional responses that have led both individuals *and* Nations into the depths of darkness, pain and suffering that endures. Need I enumerate for you to write here, exhausting your supply of paper and ink?

We also observe to our dismay, persistent Ego-possessed nay-Sayers of Human evolvement continue to govern your Earth Nations with fury and greed! Let not these be your Iconic examples of Mastery, **despite the illusion** of popular admiration of their *alleged* power, often connected with monetary wealth, contrasted with Spiritual wealth.

So, to continue restating the case for the positive, wise choices with imbedded Divine wisdom, and yes, at times coupled with Human logic, have led individuals and Nations of Earth into periods of higher vibrations of peace and love, and mutual prosperity ... ultimately producing sustained decades of joy upon certain regions of your Planet. If you have doubts, study your history, folks. Choice of conformance with Universal and Divine Law undeniably yielded these results. You are invited to join the ranks of *those who already practice emotional balance conjoined with Our wisdom,* as offered here. Mystery schools may, one day, include this rigorous healing discipline We now address, but such is not offered elsewhere at present.

This said, WE recognize and appreciate that, upon your plate, you are individually delivered a copious quantum of emotions to deal with, as you will, on a momentary, daily and on-going basis. The superior management and Mastery of your "plate of emotions" will certainly affect the *quality of your Free-will choices* as a consequence. Hence, the basic reasons for Our dissertations on this subject.

> **Your choices, then, often become imbedded *habitual behaviors,* which in turn govern your ability to achieve a higher state of vibration, and consequently, to align and commune with your Soul and Ourselves in the Ascended Realm of the Holy Spirit. To change or not to change is a Chela's clear choice, which can be chosen as bitter <u>or</u> sweet, as your perspective will allow.**

Thus, your ability to receive and <u>apply</u> Our much needed Divine guidance, on your own, as your Ego surrenders … or to receive through certain Ones of Our Channeling Vessels, … *is at stake here!* Are you with me? Re-reading the foregoing will assist.

Alright. Human emotions, inflowing as an inevitable part of your Human inheritance, will undeniably be interpreted by your consciousness in different ways, as e.g., joyful, angry, loving, laughable, challenging, tragic, frustrating, fearful, sad, hopeful, threatening, uplifting, …

Endless permutations.

These Choices are yours alone! Your Free-will choices are yours to either Master **or** to use as an indulgence in your Ego's *reactive emotional responses without consideration (satisfying as this behavior may seem in some of your moments).* This is a simple Truth! Healing is knocking at your door. You can elicit this new behavior in the wink of an eye, one emotion at a time. In a split second, a wiser than usual choice can be made to then process and handle an incoming thought. Constant awareness here is needed, and the amazing results are worth the effort!

Remember, defaulting to the unconscious reactive status quo is <u>*actually a choice*</u>, fine people. Your future in this lifetime is at stake.

We see frustration commonly giving rise to this **prevalent reactive default choice** on Planet Earth. It may be an adult temper tantrum! Or a juvenile temper tantrum, so often demonstrated! Such choices will disqualify you from the game, if this behavior is not eliminated!

So, your Portal of Entry to the Higher Realms requires fundamental change in the planes of the ordinary mind… a re-wiring of your computer, as you might say, to transmute and <u>re-record those previously planted</u> 3rd **Dimensional illusions and myths** of your belief system **into the wisdom of Divine Truth and Universal Law.** <u>We must work together</u> in partnership to deal with the **resistance that would block your transmutation to enter this Portal.**

A purified mind is a mind that can be emptied, for periods of each day, to contain the vastness of nothingness, … for ever increasing periods of time so that the hand of the Divine can reach in and caress and heal your heart, mind and body. Your ability to reach such a **Transcended state of Being,** leading to your accelerated healing process, is truly Our goal for you at this point.

Only a quiet mind can receive these higher energies. For those of you who have been in training for years and still have little or no accurate Divine listening abilities or simply very limited Spiritual intuitiveness, …. pay attention now!

There is a metaphysical reason for your being denied full access to the Divine Mind! The mass of Humanity is in this boat. The boat is sinking. Can you not see this all around you in your world?

Nonetheless, there is hope with an Action plan waiting for you. With more surrendered devotion to the process, you may later acquire ability and then be able to hear within yourself a purified mysterious "voice" from inside that can better serve you. I pray this will be the voice of Spirit <u>and not confused with the murmurings of an unaligned EGO!</u> ... a common mistake! I hasten to add that heightened intuition is also often a good first sign! Purifying your mind and quieting daily meditation(s) go hand in hand with Your ability to hear directly from Ourselves, albeit bits and pieces in the beginning.

Now, ... enters your magical opportunity to use the Spectrum of Choice (below), to practice Mastering your Emotional fluctuations. Begin now, to actively **use the guidance I present as your tool(s) of Self-insight.** You may discover that Self-correction is often more palatable than that from another. (Therefore, this writing, repeatedly embraced, will serve you well, as opposed to a simple one-time scanning, and then only to be placed in a file on your computer or resting unused upon your bookshelf!)

Then choose to consciously apply these insights to begin effectively managing and then balancing your emotional state(s). The choice is your responsibility, My Friends. ***Status quo*** seems to be the action of choice for most. What will you choose? Your Spectrum of Choice diagram is displayed below.

I heartily guide you to <u>hold this channeled dissertation carefully,</u> however you can manifest that into being. Hold Our words in your hands and partake of these Golden Gifts, and you will thank me in less than three (3) earth months of Earth-time, as new perceptions overtake your old reactive emotional patterns that have kept you stuck in the quagmire.

Gratification shall enfold you, Sweet People, believe me, as newly born *Emotional balance* resides comfortably nestled in your Being as the *companion of your quiet mind!* (When was the last time you meditated daily for 30 Earth days straight? ... or 60 days in succession?)

What do We have to do to entice you to be drawn to the Violet Flame? Yes, laziness entices the *strong-willed Ego* to take the path of least resistance at this point, conveniently holding you in its clutches, *if you allow*. <u>Strong Egos spur on the Self-indulging,</u> emotional, reactive behaviors that put you in the sinking boat, *that I point to as <u>your most common vessel of choice</u>, individually and collectively!*

The beautiful gift of Human Free-will on Planet Earth can "save the day" if you will only set *new and lasting habit patterns,* using the techniques We offer. **So, select this day as *your*** day of new beginnings for emotional balance. The Flame awaits to embrace you in its comfort, harmony and unconditional love. You can opt to be a crucial part of the progress for Mankind in your time. Your *valuable* service in Spirit is dependent upon the Mastery of this dissertation, My Beloved Ones of Light!

I await your response to Me *and* your sterling weekly report of progress in *successfully* managing your Emotions. I AM always holding *your* lighted candle in My glittering Crystal Cave of Light, shining to enfold you in My arms. Join with Me.

In unending Service of Humanity, IAM
Saint Germain and the Realm

Through *Lah Rahn Ananda* 08-31-2013

Wisdom from Above

"Upon Earth, Wisdom may be regarded as knowledge plus experience wrapped inside the Truth."

"Seek out the Joys of Change and Behold thy Friend."

"Action is the worthy companion of Hope."

"Truth is a worthy companion of Enlightenment."

"Dig deeply for rewards of The Truth, and exchange thy burdens of judgment for Freedom!"

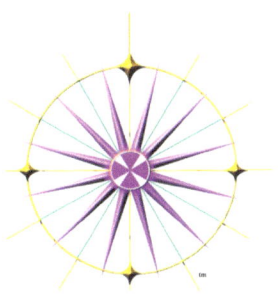

Saint Germain

Wisdom Quotations

~ 13th Edition 2004-2013

The Grand Process

The Truth

Soul Searching

Ripe Moments On The Vine

Wisdom From Above

The Grand Process

"LEFT AND RIGHT TOGETHER,

JOIN

THE ABSOLUTE AND THE RELATIVE.

REALIZED WITHIN MY BELOVED BEING,

THIS INTERNAL CONJUNCTION

BEGINS

THE MIRACULOUS BIRTH OF MY

ENLIGHTENMENT"

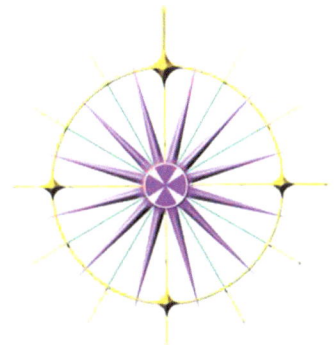

Blessings,
Lah Rahn Ananda 2013

The Truth

"Dig deeply for rewards of the truth

where Earthly illusion fades into the dusk,

and joys of freshly found freedoms

Become Yours forever."

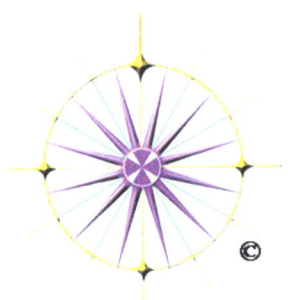 **Saint Germain** /Lah Rahn Ananda 2004

"Ripe Moments On the Vine"

AFFIRMATION FOR YOUR HARVEST

"I AM joyfully *willing* to love, care for and accept each new moment of My life as it unfolds. I acknowledge *'what is'*, and embrace the swinging door of *choice* to transcend *My* old and burdensome *judgments*.

My *life's purpose is* integrated with a clear vision of *'Change'* *as* inevitable, ... empowering Me with the Freedom to lead an *extraordinary examined life that is worth living.*"

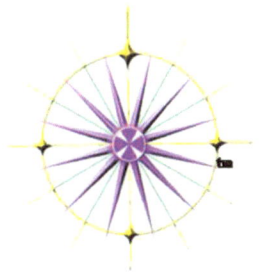

Lah Rahn / Gordon Corwin 10-2013

Soul Searching

In those dreamy and solitary moments of reflection, contemplate ... if you dare

What comes first, the Thought or the Feeling?

o

Who AM I under the mask I wear?

o

What is the focus of My Self-talk?

o

What is the Color of The Truth?

o

Rest assured, Dear Ones, your contemplations and musings are held in the vault of My Heart in the utmost confidence. Embrace your evolving reflections, as they occur over time, in your emerging and unique Grand Process.
Blessings in the Light,

El Morya *through Loli Rahn Ananda 2013*

Wisdom from Above

"Upon Earth, Wisdom may be regarded as knowledge plus experience <u>wrapped inside the Truth.</u>"

"Seek out the Joys of Change and Behold thy Friend."

"Action is the worthy companion of Hope."

"Truth is a worthy companion of Enlightenment."

"Dig deeply for rewards of The Truth, and exchange thy burdens of judgment for Freedom!"

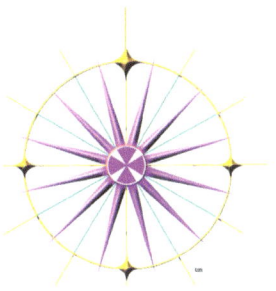

Saint Germain

Manifestation

Magic

Greetings My Beloved Chelas and Readers of casual interest as well. I come to you All. In this Fourteenth Edition of My Chronicles, I shall address the Grand Realm of Divine Magic Manifestation in two parts. To begin, let Us cast an eye together upon your Earthly business Manifestation endeavours, and take a brief glimpse at those elements you can choose to Master in this pursuit, as I shall explain.

I know that a natural Human business instinct can be creative about achieving your goals and treading this ground in the most expeditious fashion possible. For some, this route is a feverish pursuit of a free lunch. However, We understand the efficiency of taking the fewest steps, and in the shortest period of Earthly time, to achieve the desired result, yes? I have been there Myself in incarnated journeys upon Earth, in the times *before* My Soul Ascended to join other colleagues who also possessed the highest vibrations of the Ascended Realm. Back then, My little Earth life seemed complicated, when Manifestation raised its head in My minuscule and isolated personal Earthbound Universe. Now, as Divine Manifestation in Light has become My specialty, it is My stock and trade to serve, with the greatest of ease, Humans in quest of their evolvement of consciousness and, of course, of their Souls. Let Us begin.

MARKETING MANIFESTATION

~ 3rd DIMENSIONAL PLANE ASPECTS ~

Marketing Professionals face common challenges in acquiring Prospects, then converting them into Qualified Clients, and finally closing the sale with a bona fide contract.

This 3-D portion of the sequence addresses only part of the process, as the endorsement and Magical Blessing of the Ascended Realm of Spirit is also in this equation, granted or not to a Spiritual Devotee depending, in part, upon the situation's Divine alignment with Light in the eyes of Spirit. While oversimplified here, this is the sum and substance of the matter, for Ones involved in such Earthly ventures in your Duality. Be aware that Spirit surely notes the underlying, ultimate *purpose and intention* of your endeavor! You are well advised to pay heed … as *you* then seek to be paid … to the following major Marketing Phases commonly encountered in this sequential process:

Contact

Contribution

Commitment

Contract

Conversion

Closing

Commission

As you wrap your thoughts and actions around these elements of this marketing process, gift yourself by filling in your own blanks behind each distinct phase. This is up to you. Note that if a phase is omitted, ignored, or unfulfilled, your project will likely need to be started anew or just simply end. *Lessons of experience shall prevail*, fine Friends and Chelas.

Good fortune in the Light.

Saint Germain and Iah Rahn Ananda 07-2014

E shall next turn to another, and perhaps more exciting part for you, of the Manifestation phenomena where Divine Magic plays a different hand in the process, working with your consciousness, and *seemingly* requiring less 3rd Dimensional effort on your part. This dissertation will expand upon the <u>Secular framework</u> given in the preceding and limited 3rd Dimensional synopsis.

I now cordially invite you to join Me in My Etherical crystal cave of Light, brilliantly sparkling to receive you as an honoured guest in this, My lair. Although I embrace the full spectrum of Manifestation energies and Alchemy, here and today, I shall elucidate upon those particular aspects that may appear to you to be Magical, as this territory is My turf, that of the Maha Chohan Ascended Master of this Aquarian Age, enduring for the forthcoming 2000 Earth years.

Here, We come to the *Mystery of Magic*, which surrounds seemingly unexplained and delightfully synchronous events, often presented unto you by Ourselves, injected into the events of your lifestream. In the sequential unfoldment process of your Earth life, much of My Divine Magical results may be revealed to you ongoingly, like viewing one of Your Earth cinemas, unfolding a story upon your video screen.

Alright. In the flow of your Spiritual lifestream, you are charged with taking dominion over your thoughts, emotions and actions, in the same sense that as I, Saint Germain, have dominion over the territory of Manifestation from Above. Follow Me, and I will be assisting you in *your enlightenment* on Manifestation in general, as well as to gift you with many Magical events in your life, occurring from a mysterious source beyond your reach or grasp.

At the outset here, let Me distinguish between Divinely dispensed *Blessings of Synchronicity* and random good fortune, often called Serendipity.

<u>Serendipity</u> emanates from unknown random events of luck and chance, somehow showing up in Your Earth life. Many such events are regarded by Humans as being positive. Let Us say, Serendipity may be occasionally presented in your life as a special *gift from the Universe* … with no clear connection to any particular merit-worthy act or behavior on your part … a random sweet gift you receive from simply being a Human Being, alive on Earth … a pleasant gift from the Universe, helping to *balance out the Yin Yang, plus some sour parts of the duality* that you must swallow.

In contrast, however, Divine Blessings of Synchronicity are quite a different matter, as they are *intentionally dispensed* by the Ascended Masters and Angelic Realms of Spirit as particular gifts of Love, intended to evoke your trust in Spirit and to contribute joy and sweetness to a challenging Earth life. And also, to make *Our lasting presence known to you*, as *We spin and swirl Blessings of Grace*, all wrapped in positive energies, placing them into your immediate circumstances and consciousness. I would say Synchronicity is a Magical, Spiritual Phenomenon of Light and Love, intentionally sent unto you in Grace by Ourselves. Simple as that!

Some large number of Our Synchronicities go un-noticed by most of you! Many of you are asleep. Time to wake up and enjoy the ride! As you awaken and evolve, full recognition of Our Grace will become clearly obvious, … the gift itself … when We Manifest each gift … and at the very moment you receive it!

Listen and read carefully here! At the very moment you recognize you have been Gifted with a Synchronicity, consciously say to Spirit: "I AM grateful and I thank you". This is enough. We hear your voices of gratitude, Dear Friends. Partnership!

We Ascended are empowered to deliver these strokes of Magic into your daily life, and almost always, they are unexpected or surprising. The arrival of Synchronous Blessings often lifts the very hat off from the head of the astonished and bewildered One receiving Our energies. And this is good, because such Blessings cannot be called forth by you, unto yourself or to others. "Above your pay grade, you might say".

> ### *Let Me repeat. Nota Bene!*
>
> **When these magical events occur in your daily lifestream, you are wise to take heed, to recognize what has just happened, *and to take a moment of time out from your precious and personal Earthly agenda,* to express to the Creator and Holy Spirit and to the Ascended Masters, your never-ending and unconditional *gratitude* for our services and sweet gifts of amazement. Capisce? Capire?**
>
> **Your GRAND PROCESS *includes* Gratitude, Folks!**

These gifts are brought and *laid in Grace* at the feet of those of you who would be surrendered and engaged in the Trust and Truth of Spirit as your higher Reality.

As I dispense Light unto your auric field, I wave My golden scepter about in the Ethers, gathering the *quintessential energy of the moment*, which I *may* be licensed to then bring down to Earth and unto you for the enriching benefit of your conscious evolvement and perhaps into a particular circumstance.

As you become a more experienced Light Worker and surrendered Devotee of Spirit, you will begin to truly know My services in the moment and, of course, *to consciously express your newly found gratitude*, which We note well. Wise behavior for your own benefit!

For the place of Alchemy in the manifestation arena, I would point out to you that Alchemy is one subset of the whole.

We Ascended have the powers, as have certain other Aligned Beings incarnated at times upon planet Earth, to transform Earthly matter into different physical forms. Yes, We alter the molecular structure of water, for example, and suddenly out of nowhere it appears as wine. We can alter the structure of metals into different forms, as well as changing the very appearance of a living organism, altered in your reality into another organism.

You have perhaps Heard tell of My *Alchemical powers* to enter into and occupy the body of a raven, an owl, or a hawk, for example, and then to fly and sit in this form before you, allowing You to gaze upon Spirit, in that way. In this case, to gaze upon yours truly, Lord Saint Germain, temporarily incarnated to further empower you by My physical presence, … which You *desperately long to see as often as possible … and for a long duration, I might add!*

For those of you, having become awake and sensitive enough to hear My words *while I am Alchemically altered into a physical body*, you are indeed Graced. Rather, … We are both indeed Graced, by the opportunity to now interact as physical bodies, including eye contact, for a brief time.

If somewhere you experience Me in a shape-shifted form, take the pleasure of looking Me straight in the eye, if you dare! My gaze is piercing. And then, hold this gaze as long as I will allow. *Your eye contact may be the closest physical proximity you shall have in this lifetime to an Ascended Master, shape-shifted as I may be. Gaze into the eye of Spirit, and thence into the eye of your own Soul*. Do contemplate your experience in retrospect, as it will have had impact and significance.

I urge you to truly Behold these experiences, for they can be beyond description in Human words. Be wise and accept the opportunity of My offer with an open heart, … this is My gift, make it truly be yours!

Shape-shifting may all seem to you a bit far-fetched, and yet I encourage you to seek out and speak with a select few of My Spiritual Channeling Instruments, who have for years personally experienced that of which I now speak, and have shared My gaze and physical presence on numerous occasions upon Earth. Lah Rahn, if you choose. There are others.

I hasten to add, some of My same devoted Instruments have been transported out of body for periods, into the Ethers, and been in My company and that of My many colleague Masters, including El Morya, Jesus Sananda, Archangel Michael, Nada,

Portia, Hilarion, Victory, Joseph, and other Ascended Ones … all for the purpose of *directly exposing Our Instruments, in person, to the highest Octave of Vibration achievable in this parsec of Our Universe … a Sacred Space that contains fully purified energy, totally devoid of all ego, and melded in unconditional harmony and love.* This transcendent feat We have repeatedly achieved with many dedicated Ones, devoted in Our service.

Here, We have Alchemy as a subset, if you will, of the Grand Realm of Divine Manifestation. Let all of the foregoing discussion lead you to now begin standing upon the *building blocks of fundamental Manifestation in your own Earth life,* a process I have earlier discussed in these many [Saint Germain Chronicle Collection](#) pages.

From your prior reading, you will recall that the Spiritual Manifestation process involves the harmonious and *aligned interaction with Spirit and also between three fundamental Elements:*

> First, the Manifesting aspirant's ability to unconditionally surrender ego, detach from the desired outcome and align in integrity for the positive purposes of Light and goodness.

> Second, that there be an agreement in integrity and good faith between all Earthly Free-wills involved, about the object, means and methods of the Manifestation.

And Thirdly, that this particular request for Manifestation be unconditionally aligned with Divine law, Universal law and the energies of Spirit. Compliance with this 3rd element would be your endorsement, yet *not a guarantee*, depending upon fulfillment of the preceding elements. Capisce? Entende? Comprende?

As you now know, *aligned outcomes* combine the energies of all three aspects. (We often receive requests in the form of prayers; some qualify and are granted. Sadly, although considered on individual merit, many others do not pass muster nor meet standards I enforce. Does this surprise you. It is the Law.

And yes, some projects will fall through the cracks and possibly manifest, though beset by ego-driven Free-will, in convoluted form(s) nonetheless, ... out of Alignment, and without Our endorsement. Needless to say such attempts inevitably collapse, disintegrate and evaporate into nothingness, in short order! Such participants that have fallen from Grace will inevitably land in dire straits, *personally and collectively*, with very possible Karmic consequences. Think of examples!

Take My words and Gifts of Grace to heart Dear Friends, as I speak the Truth. In this 14th Chronicle Edition, you have been presented with unusual and rarely disclosed energies and elucidations, paving an *important stretch of your road to Enlightenment and to holding the 5th Dimension of higher vibration*. We in the Realm trust in your gratitude.

I AM forever in your service, Beloveds, delightfully showering down Divine and Magical Blessings of Synchronicity to those worthy Ones of you in My care. Be in joy and appreciation as you are Graced. The Nectars of which I have spoken here today, are the "frostings on your cake", Dear Friends, and the sweetness of My elixirs are ever-present to those worthy of drink from My cup. One day, We shall sup.

Be of Good Cheer, and Let Me know of your Progress, Beloved Ones.

In Light I AM,

Saint Germain

› Through Lah Rahn Ananda 07-25-14

A CLOSING NOTE, MY DEAR FRIEND

At long last, after 7 years, it is my deepest honor to present to you this First Volume of the Saint Germain Chronicles Collection, in full Spiritual Partnership with the Ascended Masters. You may want to know that this is the 3rd major book/series written and released by Ascended Master Saint Germain in the last 65 years. Also, in keeping with Saint Germain's wishes to transmit visual energies along with his Wisdom, you are now holding the first fully colour-illustrated Spiritual book of it's kind, cover to cover.

I heartfully thank you for gifting your Earth consciousness and your Soul-Self with these everlasting and timeless treasures, to support and enlighten you in your Spiritual Journey ahead … with all my best wishes.

If you would like to know more about my future fully- channeled works now in process from Saint Germain and other Ascended Masters, please contact me by email at:

Lah@SaintGermainChronicles.org

Or visit me at

www.SaintGermainChronicles.org

I look forward to hearing from you.

Love,

Lah Rahn / Gordon